SAFEGUARDING HERITAGE

A MONUMENTAL GLORY

SAFEGUARDING HERITAGE

A MONUMENTAL GLORY

Capt. Pran Ranjan Prasad

Foreword by

Dr. B. R. Mani

BHARATIYA KALA PRAKASHAN
DELHI (INDIA)

First Edition : 2008

ISBN : 978-81-8090-197-3

Published by
C.P. Gautam
BHARATIYA KALA PRAKASHAN
3421-A, IInd Floor, Narang Colony, Tri Nagar,
Delhi-110035. Phone : 32967505, Telefax: 27393083
Email : bkp3421@yahoo.co.in

Laser Typesetting by
Twinkle Graphics, Delhi-110088.

Printed by
BDH Printer at D.K. Fine Art Press Pvt. Ltd. Delhi- 52.

Dedicated to

My Parents, Wife, Son, Daughter,
Son-in-law and Granddaughter 'Suhani'

CONTENTS

प्रत्लकीर्तिमपावृणु
संयुक्त महानिदेशक
JOINT DIRECTOR GENERAL

डॉ० बुद्ध रश्मि मणि
DR. B.R. MANI

भारत सरकार
भारतीय पुरातत्व सर्वेक्षण
जनपथ, नई दिल्ली-110011
GOVERNMENT OF INDIA
ARCHAEOLOGICAL SURVEY OF INDIA
JANPATH, NEW DELHI - 110 011
Telefax : 9111-23015428, 23014821
E-mail : brmani@hotmail.com

FOREWORD

India is a repository of cultural heritage. Heritage sites and cultural remains of varied periods in our country represent the composite culture for which the country is proud about. There is a definite need to safeguard them by all means in the rapidly increasing industrial growth and deteriorating security scenario. Capt. Pran Ranjan Prasad has brought out this most important aspect to the fore through his book for everyone to understand and act in affirmation. Archaeological Survey of India is doing yeoman service in preserving and protecting the country's invaluable cultural remains. Security is one of the foremost concerns of the department. I am personally very much pleased to find that Capt. Prasad has brought out all the aspects of security of sites, monuments and museums in a most simple and explicit manner. He has not left any stone unturned in dealing with the subject in his book titled – "Safeguarding Heritage – A Monumental Glory". His in-depth knowledge and experience is aptly reflected in this book. The book explains all the aspects of management of cultural wealth from security point of view as 'Karma and Dharma'. This work is an excellent instrument for imparting training to the security personnel.

The book will certainly come handy in understanding and dealing with the matters related to security of cultural wealth even by the private collectors and trusts that are custodians of cultural remains and artifacts.

I wish him success in all his future pursuits in analyzing and devising new ways and means useful for protection of the cultural property.

23rd May, 2008

Dr. B.R. MANI
Joint Director General,
Archaeological Survey of India, New Delhi.

Indian
National Trust
for Art and
Cultural Heritage
INTACH

Prof. R.C. AGRAWAL
Principal Director
Architectural Heritage Division
71, Lodhi Estate, New Delhi-110 003
Ph. (D) : 91-11-2465 6575
General : 2463 1818, 2463 2267,
: 2463 2269, 2469 2774
Fax : 91-11-2461 1290
E-mail : intach@del3.vsnl.net.in
rcagrawal1947@gmail.com
Website : www.intach.org

Dear Captain Prasad,

I have gone through the draft of your book 'Safeguarding Heritage–A Monumental Glory' and in my opinion the security of monuments and antiquities have become one of the serious necessities in our country. This is mainly due to the interest the developed countries are taking for possessing antiquities, especially those from the oriental countries and increase of tourism. This state of affairs has led to the unlawful activities, like stealing, selling illegally and smuggling of art treasures of the ancient past and disfiguring the monuments and vandalisation by various means. The persons indulging in such nefarious activities are not foregoing or missing the slightest opportunity available. Further, security arrangements of yesteryears are no longer serving the purpose, as the thieves and smugglers are keeping themselves abreast with the modern technology.

Simultaneously, the site-museums near the monuments are also faced with the problem and the men in-charge of these museums are facing various problems arising out of this situation and devising various means to protect priceless antiquities that are kept in their charge.

The latest happening of terrorists entering in the Red Fort, unauthorized entry of people in Taj Mahal complex, anti social activities in Elephanta Caves and communalization of monuments has compelled the authorities to look into the security aspects with a new perspective and in this direction the first attempt has been made by you. Your visualization of the security concern of the monuments and artifacts with a new perspective and suggested measures, if implemented, will provide a new prospective of security cover to the monuments. I hope the analysis made by you will go a long way to achieve the security concern of the heritage of this country.

With best wishes,

Yours sincerely

(Prof. R.C. Agrawal)

Capt. P.R. Prasad,
OSD,
U.P.S.C.,
New Delhi

PREFACE

In recent years there have been tremendous increase in the unwarranted activities by the antisocial elements and criminals at the places of archaeological wealth. The artefacts have always been items of attraction and possession from times immemorial. One could find them in the princely estates and drawing rooms of rich and wealthy. Cases of theft of antiquities, misuse of archaeological sites & monuments and vandalizing cultural property are on the rise. Illicit trafficking of cultural property is a matter of great concern. Dealing in antiquities is a thriving business for the antique smugglers. The illegal trade, smuggling and other undesirable activities with reference to antiquities are a worldwide phenomenon and elements involved in such illicit trade have a well-established network with national and international connections to facilitate their nefarious activities. Although, this is a serious problem, yet irony is that, neither any security policy exists nor any hierarchal set-up even in some of those organizations that are having large numbers of security personnel on their roll. In some organizations non-professionals are dealing the matters related to security. Therefore, the security system is not on any standard pattern in such organizations. This needs immediate remedial attention. Security is a specialized subject. It is the eyes and ears of the administration of any organization. Considering the importance of this aspect, I have taken up the initiative of highlighting the main points for safeguarding our rich cultural heritage. I could take up this work because of my experience in the field and keeping in mind the fact that "Prevention is better than cure". I wish to mention here, this is a humble beginning and we must always be receptive in adopting the innovative and workable systems as well as using the state-of-the-art technology in achieving our goal. All the suggestive points in this book can very easily be brought into practice. Man management is an integral part of any organized task force. There is a general awareness in the masses regarding importance of preserving our heritage. As a result of this a number of NGOs (Non Governmental Organizations) have taken up this cause. INTACH (Indian National Trust for Art and Cultural Heritage) is one of them whose activities are spread throughout the nation. NRLC (National Research Laboratory for Conservation of Cultural Property) was established, at Lucknow in 1976 by the Department of Culture, Government of India for conservation of Cultural Property. It has a team of professionally trained conservators and conservation scientists. A Regional Conservation Laboratory (RCL) is located at Mysore. Even Archaeological Survey of India (ASI) has a project known as 'Awareness Programme' to make people aware of the importance of preservation and protection of our heritage sites and cultural wealth. People are enlightened on the preservation methodology and the importance of safeguarding them. "National Mission on Monuments and Antiquities" (NMMA) has recently been launched by the Ministry of Culture for documenting the antiquities, manuscripts and built heritage of the entire country. Even the efforts of some of the individual activists are laudable, as in the case of Victoria Memorial which has been saved from excessive pollution.

No case study of thefts and occurrences at various museums and protected sites are being mentioned in this book for the simple reason that, I do not wish to name any of them. In some cases unscrupulous role of some insiders have also come to the fore.

I am hopeful that this work would serve as a guide to the custodians of invaluable cultural remains and the security agencies engaged in safeguarding our heritage and cultural property for taking suitable actions in protecting them for posterity. Some of the points may be relevant for the museums other than the archaeological museums too. Many departments (Defence and Civil), Private Trusts and individuals are having different thematic museums. Recent one being contemplated by Delhi Metro Rail Corporation (DMRC). The management can decide on the degree to which any preventive measures are to be implemented depending on the area, location, sensitivity and the value of artefacts. Today's preventive measures would ensure preserving these treasures for the future generations. My effort has been to express myself in the simplest language, so as to be understood even by an average reader.

I feel honoured in making special mention of the names of some senior archaeologists who have always been appreciating my work. They are

Mr. C.B. Patil, Mr. S.K. Sharma, Mr. V.C. Sharma, Mrs. Sunanda Srivastava and Mr. N. Tahir all Dy. S.As; Dr. P.K. Mishra, Dr. D.V. Sharma, Mr. A.K. Sinha, Mr. K.K. Muhammad, Mr. S.J. Hasan, Mr. C.B. Mishra, Mr. M. Mahadevaiah, Mr. T.J. Baidya, Dr. D. Jitendra Das, Dr. B. Bandhopadhyay, Dr. S.V.P. Halkatti, Mr. D.N. Dimri, Mr. T.J. Alone, Dr. (Mrs.) Urmila Sant and Dr. (Miss) A. Banerjee all Superintending Archaeologists; Mr. S.B. Ota and Mr. P.B.S. Sengar both Directors. Dr. B.R. Mani, Joint Director General, Dr. G.C. Chauley and Dr. Amarendra Nath both Ex-Directors; Mr. K.N. Dikshit and Dr. R.C. Agrawal both former Joint Director Generals; Dr. (Mrs.) Debala Mitra, Dr. M.S. Nagarajarao and Mr. J.P. Joshi Ex-Director Generals, Archaeological Survey of India (ASI). Not to forget late Mr. Ajai Shanker, IAS, Director General (ASI) and Secretary to Govt. of India.

I am thankful to an array of friends and colleagues who encouraged me to undertake this work. Few of whom, I can remember now are archaeological officers Mr. Rajeev Dwivedi, Mr. Neeraj Kumar Sinha, Mr. K.C. Srivastava, Mr. Indu Prakash, Mr. P.L. Mina and Mr. Manoj Kumar Joshi. I owe special thanks to Mr. Rakesh Sharma of UPSC for rendering his services in preparing the manuscript. Mr. Suresh and Mr. Kamlesh took special care of my administrative requirements during my work.

I wish to remember some of the inspirational intellectuals from the Defence Services whose influence has always given me the determination to accomplish my task with ingenuity. They are Brig. (Retd.) M.S. Choudhary, Chief Instructor, USI; Col. (Retd.) Kulvinder Singh (Ex. Commanding Officer, 246 Mountain Regiment), Lt. Col. R.A. Prasad (Retd.) AOC, Maj. (Retd.) Bhupinder Singh Dhillon (73 Medium Regiment) and Late Maj. Gen. N. Dayal, AVSM.

My thanks are due to Dr. K.P. Poonacha, one of the very senior officers of ASI and Dr. K.M. Suresh, Director, Museum, Kannada University, Hampi for rendering invaluable suggestions from time to time and also to one of my dearest friend Mr. R.K. Verma, Archaeologist, for his suggestions on the format and for patiently going through the proof.

I feel this is the right time to bring out this publication.

Capt. Pran Ranjan Prasad

ACKNOWLEDGEMENT

ARCHAEOLOGICAL SURVEY OF INDIA

LIST OF MAPS

LIST OF PLATES

ABBREVIATIONS

AAT Act, 1972	Antiquities and Art Treasures Act, 1972
ASI	Archaeological Survey of India
CAL	Central Archaeological Library
CBI	Central Bureau of Investigation
CCTV	Close Circuit Television
CNB	Cultural Notice Board
DFMD	Door Frame Metal Detector
DMRC	Delhi Metro Rail Corporation
EBA	Endemic Bird Area
ERV	Emergency Rescue Vehicle
FIR	First Information Report
GWR	Good Work Reward
HHMD	Hand-Held Metal Detector
ICCROM	International Centre for the Study of Preservation and Restoration of Cultural Property
ICOMOS	International Council on Monuments and Sites
IISSM	International Institute of Security and Safety Management
INTACH	Indian National Trust for Art and Culture
IOC	Indian Oil Corporation
IPC	Indian Penal Code
IR	Indian Railways

IUCN	International Union for the Conservation of Nature and Natural Resources
MLR	Matheran Light Railway
NCC	National Cadet Corps
NEERI	National Environmental Engineering Research Institute
NGO	Non Governmental Organization
NMMA	National Mission on Monuments and Antiquities
NSS	National Social Service
PNB	Protection Notice Board
PRC	Punjab Regimental Centre
SITREP	Situation Report
SOP	Standard Operating Procedure
SSS	Swantantrata Sangram Sanghrahalaya
UNESCO	United Nation's Educational, Scientific and Cultural Organization
UPSC	Union Public Service Commission
USI	United Services of India
VIP	Very Important Person
WPB	Waste Paper Basket

CHAPTER 1

INTRODUCTION

Our country is one of the richest states in terms of heritage and cultural wealth. During various five-year plan provisions to preserve them by their proper upkeep, conservation and excavation for unearthing the invaluable remains of the past are being made. These heritage sites and remains are giving boost to our tourism industry. However, in the changing global security scenario these places have also become highly vulnerable to the sinister acts of the offenders. In modern times the archaeological wealth are to be guarded against sabotage, theft, damage and pilferage.

'Article – 49' of our constitution lays down: *"It shall be the obligation of the State to protect every monument or place or subject of artistic or historical interest,* ***declared by or under law*** *made by Parliament to be of national importance from spoliation, disfigurement, destruction, removal, disposal or export, as the case may be".*

Therefore, it becomes obligatory and very important duty of the State to protect the Monuments and Museums, which are institutions– *"Devoted to procurement, study, care, custody and display of objects of lasting interest and value"*.

Security of cultural wealth in its broader context means effective way to safeguard the invaluable against man-made disasters like theft, looting and riots; besides catering for emergencies through disaster planning to deal with natural disasters like earthquake, wild fire, flood, tsunami and landslide etc. Threat to archaeological wealth could be from various sources and in various forms ranging from subversion of employees' moral to sabotage, accident due to fire, civil disturbances, war and natural calamity. Generally, the bad elements indulge in looting activity at the areas affected by natural calamity, like earthquake, flood and tsunami. There should be a contingency plan to prevent this.

The responsibility of safety and security of the centrally protected monuments and museums lies totally with the ASI, as it is the chief custodian of our cultural and artistic heritage. ASI implements the provisions of Antiquities and Art Treasures Act, 1972 (AAT Act, 1972) for the protection and movement of cultural wealth. The special cell of the CBI (Central Bureau of Investigation) deals with the cases of antiquity thefts and their recovery. The term "safety and security" implies for visitors, well-being, as well. However, there are many museums and heritage sites of immense value and importance, which are either privately owned or, under the protection of various trusts and State Governments. Maps would give a picture of the presence of heritage wealth all over the country.

Large number of sites, monuments and museums are under the protection of ASI. These numbers are subject to change depending on notifications for protection of new sites and/or, de-protection of the existing ones. There are about 3667 numbers of centrally protected monuments and sites and 42 numbers of site-museums under the care of ASI, out of which 19 numbers of monuments are enlisted in the world heritage list of UNESCO (United Nation's Educational, Scientific and Cultural Organization). This entire legacy needs to be protected and preserved in their best form for the future generations to see and understand the history of glorious past of our nation. Normally monuments remain open for the visitors from sunrise to sunset. But, some of the monuments are being opened till late hours for night viewing. The role of security staff becomes more important at these monuments. A good number of monuments, sites and museums are located in the interiors of the country or, in hilly terrain, jungle and remote area. There are no approach roads and other communication facilities at some of these sites and monuments. It is, therefore, very essential to consider the strength and type of task force to protect the sites, monuments and museums thus located. Organizations have to take care of their security needs. Horticultural activities at the protected sites sometimes draw many labourers from outside who should work under proper security supervision. The security force is required to implement the security policies of the organization. They are required to be quick and responsive in dealing with the security challenges.

In recent times, rampant encroachments in and around the protected sites are posing major problems for their custodians. There is an urgent need to effectively deal with this menace. This is possible only by securing the area by physical presence of adequate number of security staff.

There is a major thrust to promote tourism in our country through "Incredible India" and "Atithi Devo Bhava" campaigns. Lately Medical Tourism is attracting people of other countries to India. It is therefore necessary to project our cultural heritage at their best.

I have coined the acronym of the word "TOURISM" as T = trouble free, O = outing, U = under, R = reasonable, I = investment for, S = sightseeing and M = merrymaking. Therefore, our endeavour should be to make it *trouble free*.

Constant search for newer and foolproof security methods are necessary to steal a march over sinister designs of criminals.

CHAPTER 2

SITES, MONUMENTS AND MUSEUMS

SITES

These are potential archaeological places, which have been protected for excavations to be undertaken in future for exposing the heritage remains. Most of them are either near some village or in remote area. It is necessary to exercise continuous full control over the entire area by its custodians. This is a very important aspect, as the residents of nearby places tend to use the land in their interest for organizing any function, sports events and for any other community utility. At some of the protected sites there is permanent thoroughfare through them connecting nearby villages and places. Vandalizing the site by unsocial elements by digging etc. cannot be ruled out. These situations are likely to pose problems in future at the time of starting any archaeological activity at these places. Therefore, it is very much essential to keep these sites well under control to avoid any unpleasant situation at any point of time. Placing of 'Protection Notice Boards' (PNB) and 'Cultural Notice Boards' (CNB) would perhaps be not enough, rather physical presence of security staff in adequate strength is the only answer to protect and exercise proper control over these sites. These sites may contain Protohistoric remains or, the remains of early historical cities.

MONUMENTS

These are heritage sites in the shape of forts, rock-cut monuments, temples, churches, mosques, heritage buildings and structural remains of immense archaeological importance. Monuments are the testimony to the excellent architectural marvels of yesteryears and reflect the history of glorious past. Each one of them differ in construction, size, layout and location; as such their security requirements are not similar. Therefore, it is very important to carry out security audit of each and every monument to ascertain their security needs. Accordingly the necessary provisioning up to satisfactory level may be made. Periodic review is necessary for upgrading and streamlining the security system by effecting the desired changes.

MUSEUMS

These are the storehouses to keep the objet d'art well protected and to display them for the visitors. The artefacts reflect the history of gone-by era. Museums are the repositories of cultural heritage and are meant for acquisition, conservation and preservation of historical, technical and other materials against decay and for their transmission to posterity as records of history. They also serve as important audio-visual means of education. The museum building should be big enough to house the artefacts and objects on display, place for conservation and chemical treatment and for research work and study. There should be proper storehouse for storing the reserve collections. The pedestals and showcases should be of perfect size, shape, material and weight to hold the artefacts and display materials properly. Showcases should have proper locking facility. There should be boundary fencing/wall around the museum and other associated buildings of proper strength, height and design with security lights. There may be a requirement of deploying armed guards at some of the museums depending on its collection, location and threat perception. The first museum-collection in India dates as long back as 1796 by the Asiatic Society which could establish a museum in 1814. The National Museum was established on 15 August 1949 in the 'Durbar Hall' of Rashtrapati Bhawan. It was formally inaugurated on 18 December 1960 on its present premises at Janpath, New Delhi.

CHAPTER 3

PROTECTIVE MEASURES

Security planning, designing and functioning would mainly depend on the following protective measures :

- Building and perimeter protection — by means of barriers, fence, wall, gates, restricted openings, security lights, surveillance and security guards in adequate strength. Construction of sentry posts and watch towers (wherever feasible). Number of duty points as per requirement.
- Control room to be organised and manned round the clock for monitoring and co-ordinating all security activities with total control all the time. Provision for maintenance and storage of firearms and other equipment. Main & duplicate key box management.
- Access control, vehicle parking area management and traffic control within the area, Entry ticket for visitors, Identity cards and passes of bona fide persons (including morning walkers inside the protected area). Labour passes, visitor book, surprise checks, proper signboards, secured storage provisions (*viz.* sculpture showcases, safe, almirah, boxes etc.).
- Ensure there are no poles or trees close to boundary wall, museum building or, the monument. Ladder, ropes, tables etc. not to be left in the open.
- Use of state-of-the-art equipments – *e.g.* siren, public address system, walkie-talkie, anti-robbery devices, close circuit televisions, smoke and fire detectors, biometric access control system etc.
- Uninterrupted power supply to be ensured. Stand-by generator and Inverter of adequate capacity must be kept in readiness all the time. Their maintenance should be carried out at regular intervals. Install solar powered electricity system, where feasible.

- Fire prevention and evacuation drills. Preventive measures against accidental outbreak of fire and its spread. Fire points located at appropriate places and equipped with right type and adequate capacity of fire extinguishers in sufficient numbers. Hydrant should be effectively functional. Water reservoir of adequate capacity, wherever necessary. Telephone numbers of local Fire Brigade Station, Police Station and Power Station to be displayed in bold letters near all the fire points and telephone sets. All the staff must know about this so that they can easily locate them during hours of need.
- Ensure serviceability of Lightning Conductors and Aircraft Obstruction Lights (if any). Ensure personnel screening, procedural controls and investigations as a preventive measure against theft and pilferage.
- **Movement of all articles and materials "*In* and *Out*" of protected area to be authorized by the competent authority as laid down in SOP. These movements must be duly recorded in the appropriate register at the Entry and Exit gates.**
- Telephone and wireless system at designated places including control room for round-the-clock communication.
- First-aid kit in the control room and at other identified points.
- Jeeps and motorcycles for patrolling and quick mobility during hours of need.
- SITREP (Situation Report) system as an essential means of information and communication between headquarters and the duty points through the intermediary offices.
- Hierarchichal chain of command in the security set up. Powers and jurisdiction delegated to the officials as per their rank for accountability, quick reaction and effective action.
- Providing security from land as well as threat from air-attack.

Security in simple terms means safeguarding heritage wealth from being lost, damaged or misused.

CHAPTER 4

SUCCESS FACTORS

1. Physical Fitness and Selection
2. Morale
3. Uniform and Kit
4. Equipment and State-of-the-Art Gadgets
5. SOP
6. Training
7. Drill
8. Strength
9. Museum
10. Duties and Area Surveillance
11. Sentry Post
12. Drinking Water and Toilet
13. Supervision and Relievers
14. First-Aid
15. Health and Hygiene
16. Liaison with Local Authorities

4.1. PHYSICAL FITNESS AND SELECTION

All the security staff should be physically fit, mentally alert and smartly turned-out. This implies fixing of criteria for selection of security personnel. There has to be laid down physical standards and recruitment tests for all the male and female candidates. They should be subjected to psychological, physical and general ability tests for judging their aptitude and fitness. Any additional skills like swimming, driving etc. may be an added qualification for selection. Sportspersons of State and National level may be given priority in selection provided they fulfil other criteria. Verification of character and antecedents must be ensured prior to their recruitment. They should undergo training after being selected, which should be aimed at making them physically fit and mentally robust. Their job should not become monotonous therefore, development and training of security personnel must be a continuing concern of the management. Security personnel must be highly motivated to give their best. There should be refresher training to keep them updated with the latest. Regular counselling at various stages is a must to ease them from stress and strain. Long and arduous duty hours does affect them adversely. Sports activities and quiz competitions etc. would help them in overcoming the monotony to a great extent. Age, training and medical fitness would be the governing factors for assigning specific nature of duty to the male and female security personnel. It is necessary to carry out medical check-up and counselling every time on their rejoining duty from leave/courses/training etc. This will keep the management abreast with their physical and mental state as well as about any socio-economic problems in order to take timely corrective measures to avoid any miss-happenings. The management should be prompt in attending to the grievances of their staff.

4.2. MORALE

Endeavour to keep the staff in high spirits works as a motivating factor. It is, therefore, very important for the security staff to be in high morale and spirit. *"All work and no play make Jack a dull boy"*. Believing on this proverb facility for outdoor games like football, volleyball etc. at select places may be provisioned. This will help in keeping them physically fit and mentally alert. It will also inculcate the sense of comradeship and brotherhood. Facility of indoor games and library may also be considered. Newspapers and good magazines may be subscribed for the staff. Television may be placed as a mode of recreation and knowledge.

Offenders may try to subvert the morale of the staff by unethical means. Management must be aware of this fact and should take timely preventive and corrective measures. For this the organization may have an internal system of keeping vigil and acquiring information about staff indulging in any nefarious activity. There should be internal system of gathering intelligence on the activity of each and every staff.

Rotation of duty place and transfer from one place to another is one of the suggested methods in ensuring that the security staff does not fall prey to allurements by local crooks. Supervision and surprise checks are also very useful ways of keeping a tag over this problem.

Provision of good work reward (GWR) to the security personnel for outstanding performance would perhaps infuse an urge to deliver their best. This is bound to boost-up their morale. There are such provisions in some of the organizations looking after the heritage sites, monuments and museums.

4.3. UNIFORM AND KIT

The uniform of security staff (male & female) should be impressive and comfortable. It should be such that the security guards must take pride in wearing them. Special care needs to be taken in selection of fabrics in accordance to the climatic conditions of the area. Cold places could be categorized into two categories viz. cold and extreme cold areas, similarly for summer season the places may be categorized into summer and extreme summer places. Selections of fabric for summer stations need special care. This is being felt necessary as in recent years definite changes in rise of temperature during summer season have been experienced. Perhaps, a phenomenon attributed to the global warming. Lightweight shoes of good quality with broad toe should be preferred for comfort in putting them on for longer duration at a stretch. Gumboots may be provided as necessitated at the identified places. Provision of raincoat, woollen short coat and woollen overcoat is essentially required for identified areas. The quantity and frequency of issue should be worked out carefully. However, the dress must not be in appearance or bearing any of the distinctive marks of the uniform of the Army, Navy, Air Force or any other Police forces of the Union or State unless approved by the concerned ministry.

4.4. EQUIPMENT AND STATE-OF-THE-ART GADGETS

It is important that the security personnel are equipped with the right type of essential equipments. Essential equipments for security are small arms, wireless communication system, Telephone, Public address system,

Siren, Back up for electricity (generator set, solar power, inverter etc.), Fire fighting equipments and need based state-of-the-art gadgets. Qualitative equipments must be procured for flawless use during hours of need. There should be provision of their storage, regular maintenance, repair and timely replacement of consumable items. All equipments should be sturdy to withstand rough and regular use for long hours without any need for quick recharge and early replacement. Periodic serviceability checks of all the equipment are mandatory. Issue and receipt of these equipments must be properly recorded. All the equipments and gadgets must be kept in order, all the time. There should be a proper system of disposal of unserviceable and condemned items. New and upgraded security gadgets may be procured as and when needed considering their utility. This will help the task force in keeping pace with the changing security threat and matching the offenders' capability. Threat analysis and vulnerability factor helps in strengthening and matching the requirement.

Right type of fire extinguishers and sensors should be placed and installed at the identified points to deal with any eventuality at any point of time. Availability of fire extinguishers nearer to the potential fire hazardous area may be ensured. Their quantity should be on the plus side so that some numbers still remain available even after few get emptied as a result of their use for extinguishing the fire. Because, refilling the emptied ones may take some time (perhaps days). Their serviceability should be checked periodically. Invariably, electrical short circuit happens to be the main cause of fire. It is therefore very important to take proper care of all electrical appliances, fixtures and wiring.

Lightning conductors must be got fixed and maintained regularly at all the museums, storehouses storing the artefacts and high rise monuments.

Aircraft obstruction lights should be got fixed at the top of the identified high-rise monuments. The serviceability of these lights must be checked on a daily basis.

4.5. SOP (Standard Operating Procedure)

What is it?

There may be different perception and approach of each individual in dealing with same problem under different circumstances on various occasions and at different places. The working capability and reaction time too differs from individual to individual. More importantly the experience of each person varies. Therefore, standardized procedures are evolved for taking appropriate actions under different situations and contingencies by the staff on duty. These procedures are known as "Standard Operating Procedure". The idea of framing SOPs is to ensure that appropriate timely action is taken in the desired degree and manner by the staff.

Mantra (Golden Rule)

The *Mantra* for drafting the *'SOP'* is *"What, Where & How"*, meaning what is required to be done at what place and how to accomplish the task. This has to be drafted by the experts of the subject based on ground reality keeping in mind various contingencies and climatic conditions (*viz.,* winter, summer, rainy, hot, humid, dry, moonlit night etc.). The required strength of staff, their skill and necessary equipments in dealing with various situations must be addressed properly while drafting the SOPs. It should be exhaustive. It must be scripted in English, Hindi and regional/local languages. SOPs are necessary for putting all the staff on one grid.

Utility

Following the Standard Operating Procedures properly and taking appropriate timely action could derive advantages in dealing with security and safety norms. The copies of the SOPs must be displayed at appropriate places. Each staff must know it by heart. Generally the SOP for a particular situation would remain same for all the places. However, situation may differ due to some valid reasons in some cases for similar eventuality, warranting necessary changes in drafting the operating procedure for such specific places. Any deviation from the SOP on its own by any staff is not warranted as it may lead to undesirable consequences. The SOPs may be reviewed periodically or as and when felt necessary by the authorities. It must be ensured that the copies of old (earlier/out-dated) SOPs are replaced with the latest one (up-dated) without any loss of time. Putting 'Effective/ Operative Date' on the SOP could ensure this. Quiz competitions could be held for keeping the staff updated and abreast with the latest provisions of SOPs. SOPs are meant for daily routine work as well as to deal with any exigency. Provisions must be scripted very clearly. For example – The desired actions to be taken in the event of any fire, misadventure by some person, looting and arson etc. Names, designation and telephone numbers of the officials and organizations (*viz.,* Police Station, Fire Station, etc.) that are to be informed telephonically or through messenger in the event of any misshappenings must be mentioned very clearly.

Maintaining 'LOG BOOK' is essentially required for recording any untoward event. This would help the authorities in investigating the causes of misshappenings and in formulating appropriate remedial measures.

4.6. TRAINING

"Practice makes a man perfect – should be the essence of good training". Basically, training means good and proficient instructors, need based training module and training environment with regards to routine and place, receptive trainee and intensive training with lots of practice. Training should be progressive and oriented towards the requirements of the site, monument and museum. They are generally categorized into 'Basic Training' and 'Refresher Courses'. Training module should vary for different levels of officials. It would be different for security guards, supervisors and managers; *i.e.* middle and senior level. Training should cover the aspects of physical training, yoga, marshal art, rock climbing, fire prevention, driving and specific to job requirements as well as contingency plans to deal with various disasters etc. Driving training should aim at making them good driver. One can become driver by learning to control the vehicle with his skill of driving, but a good driver would have to have the sense of anticipating the wrong move or, the foolishness of others to avoid any accident. Hill driving is a special type of skill. All drivers should be subjected to periodic mandatory health check-up, especially for night vision and reflex action.

Case studies of miss-happenings at other places may give an idea of implementing and adopting new and innovative preventive methods. Training should aim at motivating every security guard to display courage far beyond the call of duty in highly adverse situations. Situation reaction ability would be the hallmark to success. Their courteous behaviour towards the visitors is very much desired. They may be given training of ceremonial drill. Well trained and highly motivated guards would be capable of delivering their best.

Training programme should normally cover the following aspects:

- Heritage Orientation and Indoctrination.
- Input about the opening and closing timings, as well as the closing days of the sites, monuments and museums.
- Detailed knowledge about the charges for entry tickets, camera etc. at the ticketed sites, monuments and museums.
- Checking procedure of Identity cards and passes etc.
- Anti sabotage checking, first aid, fire fighting, self-defence and unarmed combat.
- Provisions and laws regarding Indian Penal Code, Police powers of arrest, search and seizure etc.
- Training for proper telephonic communication, generating SITREP (Situation Report) and lodging of FIR (First Information Report) etc.
- To remain polite but firm, specially while dealing with the visitors.
- Handling of arms and equipment.
- Driving of different types of vehicles.
- Updated knowledge and training as per SOP (Standard Operating Procedure).
- Inculcating interest and dedication towards duty.

Mock exercises should be conducted as part of keeping the security staff alert and for gearing up their effectiveness in dealing with various contingencies at short notice. Number of contingency plans to deal with fire and other exigencies should be practiced. Workshops and seminars should be organised periodically for imparting information about latest procedures, systems and equipment. Some relevant case studies of dealing with cases of fire, miss-happenings and thefts etc. could be discussed and analysed in order to gain knowledge. This would help in formulating own security module. There should be provision to impart specialized training (*viz.,* Bomb detection and defusing, drill against terrorist attack etc.) to the security personnel.

4.7. DRILL

Practicing security and fire prevention drills would give a chance to every security personnel to know the actions to be taken by them during different situations at various places. These drills should be practised during day as well as at night and on adverse climatic conditions too. This practice may be carried out at least thrice a year on a large scale and once in two months in small scales, so that every security staff gets an opportunity to participate as many times, since at some period of the year they may be on leave, training etc. They would be practically handling various types of extinguishers and performing different roles of safety and security. Security guards must familiarise themselves with the area and their specific duty. It is very important for them to know the terrain they have to operate in. The role of fire fighting party is to douse the fire, save & salvage life & property and to cordon off the area to prevent mischief by the bad elements. Bad elements try to loot the affected area.

4.8. STRENGTH

The strength of security personnel is required to be worked out for each and every heritage site, monument and museum. While working out the strength it must be borne in mind that a sentry on duty can perform the duty of watch and ward to the degree and ability he/she can handle. Thereafter, there would be a requirement of additional security staff to deal with the situation, if so warranted. Nothing can be done at the eleventh hour if the organization is not prepared for it well in advance. Some staff may be on leave or, sick. If the staff quarters are close to their duty place then their availability at short notice could be a boon for the department. Success will depend on ensuring that at no stage should the offenders outnumber the security staff.

"Security should be based on vulnerability analysis by experts through an in-depth examination of the probabilities of occurrences of various risks based on factors like physical environments, procedures, and past history of thefts and other problems etc."

So, the parameters for working out the strength are as follows :

(*a*) Threat perception based on previous happenings (if any), layout, importance and the total area of the protected place.

(*b*) Identify duty points for day and night and requirement of number of patrolling parties.

(*c*) Identify nature of duty at each of the duty points (*viz.* security control room, entry & exit gates, ticket counters, fire duty and patrolling duty).

(*d*) Security considerations during VIP visits, Cultural festivals within or nearby protected area, Filming operations and other such exigencies (*i.e.* National/State/Local functions, civil disturbance, riots, mob fury etc.).

(*e*) There is a need of deployment of adequate strength of security personnel (male and female) during rush hours at the entry point, exit point, ticket counters and at select points to regulate the movement of visitors. It should be borne in mind that the visitors have their own itinerary and time schedule; therefore, wastage of time does matter to them. They might have hired the taxi for a limited period to visit as many monu-ments in a short span of time. Therefore, our endeavour should be to facilitate them in this by letting them go through all the procedure without much delay. Why should there be rush at any particular point, may it be ticket counters or the security checkpoints.

(*f*) Specific kind of security is needed at the identified monuments and museums as per their importance and sensitiveness. World Heritage Monuments and the museums housing precious artefacts fall in this category. Their locations would also be a factor of consideration.

4.9. MUSEUM

All the parameters of a proper museum building can be taken care of while constructing new building for the museum. But, many museums are housed in ancient buildings. It is therefore very essential to survey these buildings from security point of view. The structure of museum building and the store must be in perfect condition. There should not be any seepage and the walls and roof must be in perfect state. There should not be any other structure adjacent to them. They should be free from dampness. Necessary precautions must be taken against pesticides, rats and birds etc. All antiquities and artefacts should be kept at the safe places protecting them even from nature's vagary. Lightning conductors must be fixed at the top of all the museum buildings. All electrical fixtures and wirings should be in proper condition. There should be sufficient illumination in and outside the building. Required number of fire preventive and fire fighting provisions must be made at identified locations. Hydrant may be a necessity for big museums. All showcases, galleries, rooms and entrance/exit doors must have proper locking facility. Documentation of all the museum objects must be made in the 'Accession Register'. All the objects must bear their accession numbers. Movement of the objects from one place to another must be duly recorded in the appropriate register. Reserve collections must be properly kept in the strong room or, the store. Due care is needed to be taken while cleaning and handling the artefacts. All this and any repair work in the museum should be carried out in the presence of some responsible person. There may be a requirement of having armed guards at some museums. The well protective boundary and gates should be of proper height and design. There should not be any pole, tree or structure close to the boundary or the museum buildings. From security point of view it is recommended that there should be only one entry and exit gate for the museums. The doors and gates must be opened and closed at the prescribed timings by the authorized personnel. The locks required to be sealed after locking should be earmarked. They should be sealed properly after locking and de-sealed before unlocking. However, the intactness of the seal should be checked before opening the lock. In case of any doubt the lock should not be opened and the matter reported to the authorities as per the SOP. The officials while operating the keys from the key box must make entry in the register. Necessary security gadgets should be installed at the entry, exit and other identified places. All postal packages received either through post or courier must be subjected to security screening for any explosive devices. In general term they are called postal bombs. Visitors must be regulated during rush hours to avoid crowding inside the museum galleries. The entire area must be sanitized everyday after opening and before closing the museum to ensure that there are no unauthorised persons or unattended article. Last but not the least, proper handing/taking-over should be carried out between the officials by physically counting the antiquities and collections.

4.10. DUTIES AND AREA SURVEILLANCE

The duty of the security staff at the heritage site and museum is somewhat different than the normal security duties elsewhere. This is because the visitors from across the globe are allowed to throng the place. In such a situation the nature of security duty calls for extra vigil and control. Basically, the role is regulatory in nature. Moreover, the visitors are free to roam about the area at their will from opening till closing hours. Therefore, the duty points of security staff should be so located that the entire area should remain under their visual observation. Carrying out patrolling of the periphery and the inner area by day and night should further substantiate this. These patrolling parties must immediately report to their control centre on noticing any unusual happenings. They are generally required to ensure intactness of the boundary wall and fence and to keep watch on the area for any suspicious article or unusual activity. They must make sure that the area is free from any unauthorized persons and cattle. Installation of security lights and qualitative state-of-the-art-gadgets may be necessary for surveillance and access control. Security personnel must be absolutely clear about their role. Duty of opening and closing the main gates and doors and to switch 'ON' and 'OFF' the security lights must be entrusted to the guards of the specific duty points. They must keep strict vigil on the garbage pickers. Guards and the patrolling party should remain in communication with the control room. System of transmitting SITREP (Situation Report) up the chain is essentially required in any security set up. The controlling authority should analyse the SITREP and act accordingly. The set-up must be geared up to deal with extraordinary situations at any point of time. **"Stitch in time saves nine."** Contingency plans to deal with the extraordinary security situations must be chalked out and practiced well. These may be the one in which more strength of security personnel and special equipments would be required. Support from local administration may be necessitated under the circumstances. The validity of Identity cards/entry passes/tickets of the visitors must be checked at the entry point. Vehicles with authorized entry passes should only be allowed to enter the permissible protected area. However, vehicles with unrecognisable registration number should not be allowed inside, even if they have the vehicle entry pass. Bona fide of all the persons travelling in the vehicle (two wheeler/four wheeler) must be verified at the entry point.

Generally, the visitors find the heritage sites usable the way they wish to. It is the duty of the security staff to discipline them and ensure that the sanity of the heritage site is maintained. Neither should they be allowed to engrave graffiti on the monuments, nor to misuse the premises in an unsavoury manner.

"The security staff needs to be polite but firm and tolerant while dealing with the visitors".

Basically, the nature of duty of the security staff can be divided into two parts– *External* and *Internal*. External means duty at the entry & exit points, vehicle parking area and the periphery, while internal means keeping vigil on the area within the boundary as well as inside the museums and other buildings. The lifts, stairs and roofs must also be under surveillance. Sometimes visitors forget their belongings in the premises. As and when found, they should be deposited in the office and kept safely so that they could be handed over back to its claimant after verification. There should be provision of locker facility in the properly managed cloakroom at the appropriate locations. Cloakroom should not be close to the museum building or the stores. The safety and security of the visitors too are of prime importance, as such, it should be mandatory to ensure that the area is free from stray dogs, monkeys and other animals. At some cities zoological parks are located in immediate vicinity of the protected monuments. It has practically been seen that a single '*Langur*' makes the herd of monkeys flee. This is effectively being practiced at many places for keeping their area free from monkey menace. Beehives are very common sight at the high-rise structures and trees. These must be watched carefully and necessary precautionary measures must be taken. At times, unruly crowd for some reason or the other create problems. The security personnel must be prudent in dealing with such situations. Mob mentality culminates into peculiar and unpredictable behavioural actions. The security guards must check trespassing and encroachment.

It is desirable to seek the opinion of security experts at the inception stage while planning construction of any new building or structure etc. This will help the organization in taking care of the security aspects right from the initial stages.

The security personnel must be placed on duty at the areas where labourers are put to work, near generator sets and at the places where arrangements are made for any functions to be held within the protected area. They must keep vigil on the arrangements and setting-up of stage & spectators' gallery and their approach. Invariably it has been seen that the preparations made during day light sans the precautionary arrangements for night.

Sanitizing the area from security point of view before any function must be a top priority for the security forces.

4.11. SENTRY POST

Sentry posts are required at all such duty points where there is no overhead cover. These posts must provide adequate protection from sun and rain. The size and design of the sentry posts should be big enough to accommodate the required number of security personnel and provide proper working space. Electrical and electronic fixtures (telephone & inverter etc.) should be provided as per requirement. The sentry posts should be so designed that the guard can have unobstructed view of its surroundings (area of responsibility). Bulletproof posts with or without periscope may be provided at the identified places. Their design and colour should match the surrounding structures.

4.12. DRINKING WATER AND TOILET

It is very important that the security guards consume safe and clean water even while on duty. Therefore, necessary provisions are required to be catered-for in this regard. They should be provided with water bottles and drinking water storage facility. A well maintained toilet in the nearby area is essentially required. These provisions would take care of their health.

4.13. SUPERVISION AND RELIEVERS

Supervision is the essence of any effective task force, be it security or, any other field. Supervision helps in keeping the staff alert and the management updated with the progress of work and other happenings. It is therefore very essential to have a hierarchichal structure in the security set-up.

It is necessary to give relief to the guard on duty at intermittent period for meals and other necessities. Therefore, there should be provision of a reliever in the duty roster. Duty hours of sentry should justify the person's endurance. Every individual has a different potential and capability to perform. This should be identified and an all out effort should be made to place the staff on duty accordingly. Age, experience and expertise of a security person (both male and female) may be considered as further requirement for the particular duty place. Change over of sentry duty must be preceded with necessary briefing and area familiarization.

Until the work is checked it should not be taken for granted that it is done.

4.14. FIRST - AID

Provision of 'First-Aid Kit' and training to all the personal is very essential. This should be part of initial training as well as refresher courses. Telephone numbers of doctors, nearest clinics and hospitals should be painted in bold letters on all the 'First-Aid' boxes. This will come handy during hours of need. These telephone numbers must be updated as and when they get changed or, any new telephone is installed. It will be nice if their location chart is displayed at an appropriate place.

4.15. HEALTH AND HYGIENE

Good health is the essence of happy living. Therefore, it is very essential for all, particularly the security personal to take care of their personal hygiene, sanitation and health. It is, therefore, necessary to give adequate time to them for attending to their health and hygiene requirements. Health card of each individual must be maintained and their blood group and information about allergy from any medicine (if known) must clearly be mentioned in bold letters with red ink at the appropriate column, preferably on the first page of the health card. Health card may either be kept in the office or, it may be with the individual if posted at far-flung isolated sites. Health card must be placed before the doctor each and every time the person goes for medical consultation. It is necessary that they undergo periodic mandatory medical check-up. They must report to the doctor on falling ill or, for any other medical problem. Blood group of all the staff must also be available in the office and the control room. This will facilitate the management in identifying the persons of a particular blood group for blood donation to their fellow person, in the event of such a contingency.

4.16. LIAISON WITH LOCAL AUTHORITIES

It is very much desired that the security officials maintain close liaison with the local administration, police, fire station, electricity and water supply office. This is required for seeking their services during hours of need. They should be kept informed about any function or activity being organized at the site, monument and museum while requisitioning their services.

Accountability, monitoring, giving right direction is the purpose of having chain of command.

CHAPTER 5

MANAGEMENT TIPS

5.1. STATE-OF-THE-ART TECHNOLOGY

Equipments are the tools to assist an individual perform well to the desired level of efficiency. Some of them are hardware tools while others are sensitive electronic equipments. These are called state-of-the-art equipments. Need based use of these equipments must be made in the desired manner, mode and quantity. These equipments could be burglar alarm, smoke and heat detectors, close circuit television, biometric access control system, public address system, electronically operated turn style gates and road barriers etc. Their functional efficiency must always be checked and upgraded as and when required.

5.2. LOCK AND KEY MANAGEMENT

From security point of view only good quality locks of branded company should be used and officials should be nominated and made responsible for the custody and operation of the key boxes. There should be one press-type of lock for locking the duplicate key box only, while all the other locks should be of the type that could be opened and locked with their keys only. Under no circumstances should the location of the locks be interchanged. Entry should be made in the register of each lock with their number and location. Some spare locks of proper size should always be available with the authorities. Whenever any key or, the lock gets defective then these must be replaced with new one rather than getting them repaired. Duplicate keys should never be got made if the keys get lost or become inoperative due to any reason. There should be an 'Original Key Box' and a 'Duplicate Key Box' having glass covers with locking facility. These days each lock is being provided with a set of three keys. In this case, two keys of each lock should be kept in the duplicate key box, while one should be used and kept in the original key box every time after its use. Duplicate keys of every lock and all the keys of the press type lock for locking the duplicate key box should be kept in the duplicate key box. Pressing the lock should lock the duplicate key box after putting all the keys of the lock of duplicate key box and all the duplicate keys of the locks in use. Under no circumstances should the keys be in the possession of any officials. When required, the glass pane of the duplicate key box should be broken to get the duplicate keys. Only extraordinary situation would warrant this action. The broken glass pane should then be replaced with the new one at the first instance. The locks should be replaced with a new one even when the numbers on the key gets obliterated beyond recognition. The rejected locks and keys must be destroyed and disposed off. No one other than the storekeeper or, the authorised person should have the access to these rejected locks and keys until disposed off. Necessary entries must be made in the register of their disposal.

The letterboxes, suggestion boxes etc., must be kept unlocked during VIP visits and major functions. This is advisable so that these boxes could easily be searched by the security agencies in the event of some explosives or, detonating devices being put in them by some mischief-monsters.

5.3. PARKING AREA MANAGEMENT

It is very important to maintain and manage the parking area. Trained personnel should man the parking area. Personnel must be trained as Traffic Marshals on traffic management. The area should be well secured and free from garbage. It should not be very far from the entrance to the protected sites, monuments and museums. The parking place should not be waterlogged and its entry and exit should be clear of any obstructions. If required, barriers may be put at entry and exit points. Preferably there should be shed and rest bays for the drivers-on-waiting and the staff. Drinking water facility must be provisioned in the area. Sufficient numbers of right type of 'Fire Fighting Equipments' should be placed at fire points in the area. Well-maintained public convenience close to the area is desirable. Parking area should be well illuminated at night. The guards on duty must have 'Trolley Mirrors' with them for inspecting the bottom portion of the vehicles for any suspect material. No vehicle should be allowed to remain overnight in the parking area. The vehicles should be guided properly to their parking slot by the staff on duty for maximum utilization of the area. Signboards should be placed indicating the parking areas for Bicycles, Two-wheelers, Cars and Buses etc. The area must be kept neat and clean as well as free from cattle, stray dogs and encroachment. There must be departmental control over the contractors in case the parking area has been leased out. It should be ensured that the staffs of the contractor are very well trained to use the 'Trolley Mirrors' and 'Fire Fighting Equipments'. They must know the "Do's & Don'ts". Department should have the provision of issuing identification stickers for bona fide vehicles. The validity of these stickers may be for one calendar year. The shape, size, colour and design may be kept different for each year for easy recognition. Vehicle stickers should be issued to the owner on production of the registration certificate of their vehicle. All the vehicles should be parked at the owners' risk along with all the belonging in it and necessary signage or notice boards in this regard must be placed at the appropriate places. However, services of cloakroom may be utilised for keeping their belongings wherever such facility is available.

5.4. SIGNBOARDS & NOTICE BOARDS

This is very important to help the visitors in giving relevant information about "Do's & Don'ts" and informing them about various locations. Therefore, the signage must be placed at conspicuous points. These could be in bold letters in English, Devnagari and the local script (if any). All signages including protection notice boards, cultural notice boards, tariff details etc. should be fixed at eye level of a person of average height for ease in reading them. However, some boards could be placed at some height with bold letters for reading them from a distance. This will depend on the judgement of the authorities as per the layout of the place. Colour choice of paints or, radium letters would depend on the management as per requirement. Periodic checks should be carried out to ensure that they are in proper condition. However, immediate attention should be paid in rectifying them, no sooner any deficiency is noticed. Delay in rectification may cause embarrassment to the management and the department, since the visitors carry the impression about any place as they have seen or experienced and seldom would a person revisit the place to see things after the mistake has been set right.

5.5. FUNCTIONS AND FILMING OPERATIONS AT HERITAGE SITES

A number of festivals are celebrated at different monuments as an annual function. Besides, a number of functions are organised by various agencies within the premises of the protected area as per the permission granted by the competent authority. Similarly, permission is granted to the individuals or agencies for filming operations within the protected area. During all the above occasions a number of activities take place for several days from preparation till its conclusion. This entails movement of personnel, materials and transport. Security personnel must ensure their smooth movement and arrangement as per the clauses in the permission letter granted to them for the purpose and duration. Security staff must impress upon the permission holders to adhere to the security norms. Security surveillance at the main places (near VIP enclosure, electricity generator set, refreshment area and other enclosures etc.) should be beefed up to avoid any miss-happenings. Fire-fighting equipments should be placed near the venue of these functions. As per the necessity, the services of fire brigade may also be requisitioned well in advance.

5.6. CONTROL ROOM

This is the nerve centre of any security set-up functioning round the clock as the control point. Only the experienced and well-versed staffs should man these centres. The role of any control room is to provide advisory as well as functional support to the guards on duty within its jurisdiction during hours of need. The control room should be well organized to allow the required number of staff to function with ease. It must remain in constant communication with its entire outposts, local police station and the administration. There should be adequate numbers of telephone and other communication facility, clock, massage logbooks and electrical and electronic systems. At times situation may warrant availability of vehicles in readiness with drivers on duty at some control centres.

Proactive actions are preventive while reactive are investigative.

CHAPTER 6

TOTAL SECURITY

This means not leaving any security action or drill to chance either by mistake or unintentionally. Thereby, it is desirable to train the staff well and standardise the sequence of security checks. Standard Operating Procedure (SOP) should be well drafted for the site, monument and museum to cater for their specific requirements. Supervision at all levels is necessary to ensure flawless performance of the staff and the security system as well as ensuring their accountability. The responsibility of issuing of permanent or temporary Identity Cards, Gate Passes and Vehicle Passes should be that of the security wing. Preferably all the individual's passes should have their passport size or, stamp size photographs, while the vehicle passes should have the photograph of the vehicle with its number plate. Frisking of individuals should be conducted from head to toe. Items like purse, bags, bottles, umbrella, walking stick, torch, toy, camera, mobile phone, walkman, music system, pen, books, other published materials, wheel chairs, waste paper baskets (w.p.b.) and any other suspect articles must be thoroughly checked. At times it may be necessary to get the plastered body parts of any suspect visitor checked by metal detectors etc. Checking invariably implies physical check, use of HHMD (hand-held metal detectors), DFMD (door frame metal detectors), X-ray machines, CCTV (close circuit television) and trained dogs. Control room of CCTV should be very well secured. Entry to the control room should be restricted to the bona fide personnel only. Deployment of trained dogs should be done under the care of its handler for short durations and for specific purpose. Its services should not be extended for general area surveillance round the clock. Security consciousness should be equal for all ranks. Security checks and restrictions must be carried out without any exceptions and irrespective of status of the person concerned. Therefore, senior officials and security personnel should voluntarily subject themselves to mandatory security checks as part of routine discipline. Degree of security checks of the visitors and their belongings would vary as per the circumstances and requirement. It would also differ from place to place depending on the availability and facility of screening and scanning gadgets. The intensity of checks would be different from routine check on normal days to thorough checks during VIP visits and on high alert days. We should not loose sight of the fact that ultimately it is the man behind the gun who scripts the success story. Therefore, it should be understood that the equipments and gadgets are only means to help the well-trained user in reacting quickly to deal with the situation appropriately. Required strength of manpower is needed to protect any heritage site and artefacts by their physical presence. Success would depend on surveillance of the entire premises of the area of responsibility, frisking and scanning of visitors' belongings and activation of alert alarms at right moment to draw the attention of the authorities and law enforcing agencies.

Laxity in security drill does not give another chance to rectify the lapse. There should not be any compromise in alertness and degree of dealing with the situation effectively. It should be borne in mind that the offenders keep looking for an opportune moment to strike. The endeavour of the security task force should be to disallow them any such opportunity. However, it is very important that the security guards do not loose sight of their own safety measures while dealing with the offenders. *There is nothing known as permanent solution in the security parlance*. There is nothing like success which succeeds in whatever manner it comes. Therefore, keeping pace with the changing security scenario in dealing with new and innovative methods of threat by the offenders is the call of the hour. Goal of the security task force should be – "*Constant search for newer and foolproof security methods to steal a march over sinister designs of offenders*".

From the modern management point of view, organizing security functions in any department involves planning, establishing controls, organizing security branch by employing professionals, good training, effective supervision, setting security procedures and making periodical departmental reviews and evaluation of security procedures for necessary changes as and when required. Once the security goals and responsibilities for the security force are identified then the task of this force would be to identify the potential areas of threat and to accordingly develop and install appropriate security measures. Security personnel should be able to pre-empt any untoward happenings. "*Threat assessment and threat evaluation is a highly professional task*". Organization should be fully geared up to implement the desired changes without delay towards improvement of security functioning.

System approach to heritage security should cater for the following:

- Organized security set-up with hierarchichal chain of command.
- Ensure availability of required strength of trained security personnel.
- 'Security Audit' at the desired intervals for evaluation of risks and dangers.
- Risk analysis.
- Good customized training.
- Imparting knowledge of 'Do's & Don'ts' as per Acts & Rules.
- Establishing security procedures and controls as per Security Manual and SOP (Standard Operating Procedure).
- Ensuring availability of right type and qualitative physical hardware and electronic devices in adequate quantity.
- Good communication is the hallmark of an effective security system.
- System of passage of information to public and within the department should be precise and within split of second.
- Ensuring implementation of security schemes and carrying out their periodic review.
- Necessary changes in the system to be brought about without delay, as and when required.
- Task force to be 'Quick and Responsive".

Quick decision, immediate implementation
and
flexible in approach are the hallmark of success.

CHAPTER 7

IMPORTANT POINTS FOR THE SECURITY TASK FORCE *(STAFF AND MANAGEMENT)*

1. Round the clock security umbrella to be provided to the entire protected area.
2. Trained security personnel to man all the duty points in satisfactory strength.
3. Security guards should not be put on any sundry duty. This may not only distract them from their main duty but they may take advantage of this in the event of any lapses by them in security duty.
4. Guards to be in pairs at night duty.
5. Change over of duties, as well as relieving duty must be carried out properly and communicated to the control centre.
6. All security personnel must be clear about their duties and responsibility.
7. All equipments and transport etc. should be maintained and kept in serviceable condition all the time.
8. While on duty, all the security staff should remain in communication with their control room round the clock. Control room to maintain logbook.
9. 100% frisking and checking of visitors and their baggage should be carried out.
10. Security staff must use metal detectors and trolley mirrors as and when required.

11. There should be an SOP (standard operating procedure) for cloakroom management.
12. Adequate security must be ensured during morning hours at the protected area where bona fide morning walkers are being permitted.
13. Pets should not be allowed in the heritage sites and protected areas at any point of time.
14. Ensure security and safety of visitors.
15. Vehicles carrying materials In and Out of the area must be thoroughly checked and searched. Entry must be made in the movement register.
16. No unauthorized personnel or vehicle be allowed in the protected area at any point of time.
17. Any suspicious act or movement by any visitor or person must be challenged, apprehended, reported and handed over to the law-enforcing agency.
18. Adequate number of CCTV cameras should be installed so that the entire area is covered in their view.
19. CCTV should have the recording facility for the duration of at least three months. Because, invariably any miss-outs come to the knowledge of the authorities only after some days or weeks. Thereby footage of at least three months would help the investigating agencies.
20. Adequate number of trained staff should be put on duty to continuously monitor the CCTV screen. Even the staff on night duty should have a glance at the screen from time to time as a routine check.
21. Security alarm system must be kept in order all the time. Their serviceability must be checked periodically duly informing the local police.
22. The requirement of different types of fire fighting equipments must be assessed and placed at the appropriate locations. Their serviceability must be checked periodically.
23. The contents of all the First-Aid boxes must be checked regularly. They must be complete and kept in readiness all the time.

24. Security staff must be vigilant and should report about any untoward incident noticed by them immediately to the control centre and higher-ups as per the SOP.
25. All important documents and accession registers etc. must be kept in safe custody.
26. The management must be geared up for quick and responsive actions as per requirement, during hours of need.
27. All the officials and staff must be clear about the actions to be taken in the event of any untoward happenings or any security lapse.
28. Regular medical check-up and counselling of all the staff is necessary, especially after rejoining from leave/vacation/training etc.
29. Management should see that the functional requirements of their security staff are met in time so as to ensure that their physical fitness and mental state is good and morale very high.
30. Regular supervision at all levels up the chain of command is essential for ensuring smooth and effective functioning of the security system and for ensuring their accountability.
31. Security task force is required to ensure implementation of relevant policies of the management and the organization in its totality.
32. There should be no gap between intelligence input and taking necessary measures. Intelligence warnings should not be ignored.
33. "Safety Awareness Week" may be organized for general public.

Foolproof security means well-trained personnel to be properly equipped and effectively supervised.

CHAPTER 8

ROLE OF SCIENCE BRANCH AND EPIGRAPHY BRANCH OF ASI

Science Branch

This branch deals with the chemical preservation of the monuments and artefacts made of various materials such as stone, metal, terracotta, bone, shell, ivory, wood, textiles etc. The office of the Director (Science) is located at Dehradun (Uttarakhand). There are a number of Zonal offices across the country including Air Pollution Monitoring Laboratory at Agra.

Epigraphy Branch

This branch deals with the study of the text of ancient inscriptions such as stone inscriptions, manuscripts on various mediums and on coins etc. They decipher them even by taking stamp ages. They study the style, dates that are given on the inscriptions/manuscripts reflecting the period they are assigned to and thus knowing the authentic history, economy, religion and social structure of any society during that period. It is necessary to understand their meaning for relating them with the history and period of that place and/or event etc. The Office of the Director (Epigraphy) at Mysore, Karnataka looks after the work of Sanskrit and Dravidian languages while the Office of Director (Epigraphy) at Nagpur is for Arabic and Persian languages. There are two zonal offices located at Chennai (Southern Zone) and Lucknow (Northern Zone).

CHAPTER 9

CAUTION AND PREVENTION

Certain precautions are needed while dealing with the matters related to security, especially in the case of cultural property. Many types of services are being outsourced these days by a number of organizations. Security services are also one of them. But, a word of caution is needed to be sounded on the following grounds in case any organization is contemplating to requisition the services of private security agencies for the protection of invaluable cultural wealth. Some of the security agencies employ guards without getting their antecedents verified through police. There is no system of carrying out their psychological and detailed medical tests. Many agencies do not have any system of imparting proper and customized training to them. Many a time the guards are put on extra duty by their employers due to shortage of staff, which is bound to affect their efficiency. In most of the cases the private security agencies neither have guards on their permanent roll, nor do they have any training centre. These agencies invariably have the contractual clause of terminating the services of the erring guards if found guilty or deficient in their duty. This may not be enough to satisfy the client. Moreover, what would be the remedial proposition in the event of security agency's staff resorting to strike for any grievance against their employer or the agency-declaring lockout? Also, there is a probability of some of the private guards falling prey to the tricks and allurement of the antique smugglers. Therefore, it is very important for the organization to consider these factors before entering into such a contract with any private security agency. Necessary clauses must be incorporated in the contract to safeguard the interest of the hiring organization. It should also be borne in mind that at no point should these agencies be allowed to operate independently at any of the heritage sites. It should be mandatory for the outsourced staff on duty to display on their uniform the identification badge of the client organization. Sometimes, security personnel of various agencies are put on duty at one site. In such a situation it is very important for the client organization to exercise effective control over all of them with regard to defining their jurisdiction and duties to avoid any confusion. Moreover, it must be understood that the outsourced agencies would try to avoid reporting about any of their lapses for fear of getting bad name or loosing the contract. They would also try to palm off (Buck-passing) any lapse towards other agencies. This may be detrimental for the client organization. Therefore, it is very important that all the security agencies must function under the client's supervision. As far as practical multiplicity of security agencies at one site must be avoided. Ideally big organizations must have their own security force having security experts in the hierarchy. In any case the requirement of security guards at the heritage sites and museums is of permanent nature, therefore if there is a dedicated specialized task force ("Heritage Protection Force") exclusively for the purpose then there will not be any additional workload on other security forces and local police to provide manpower out of their strength.

It should be incumbent on the part of the organization to include the security experts in the security policymaking of the organization. Well-thought and well-planned security proposals would prove to be very effective and fruitful.

Security staff on duty to be firm but polite while regulating visitors.

CHAPTER 10

CONCLUSION

Security in general term means not to loose one's possession by ensuring the required security measures. It will depend on the threat perception and analysis. Preventive measures would base on the degree and nature of anticipated threat. Moreover, it is not only the man made external threat which is responsible for any loss, but even the protective provisions and the places where they are kept would have to be perfect to prevent any such occurrences. Allout efforts should be made not to provide any opportunity to the offender. Providing security is a round-the-clock effort, while only one occasion is required for the offenders to succeed in their sinister acts. Bearing this in mind there should not be any laxity in the security norms. Security personnel must be physically fit, trained well and equipped with the right type of equipments and gadgets. The security requirement of each and every heritage site, monument and museum are different. Thereby, the security norms would vary according to the requirements of the particular place. Again, necessary changes would have to be adopted as and when warranted, due to change in security scenario. Life of every human being is precious, so is of trained security personnel. Therefore, our endeavour should be to make use of the gadgets and equipments for surveillance, detection of explosives and movement of personnel and in countering any sinister acts of the offenders. Effort should be to minimise risk on our side. Our endeavour should be not to get caught unawares. Security personnel should be geared up to meet any challenges effectively. Air pollution and vibrations due to low flying aircrafts and use of dynamite and other explosives for mining does affect those monuments, which are in close vicinity. Pollutants get accumulated and cracks develop on the monuments due to this. Necessary steps should be initiated through the concerned agency to take remedial steps. Safeguarding heritage property certainly brings in a lot of joy as it gives a sense of satisfaction in contributing towards protecting the nation's cultural treasure.

Relevance of rules, regulations and acts can be justified only if there is a task force to ensure their implementation. Merely framing of rules, regulations and acts, however stringent they may be and putting up protection notice boards would not serve the purpose unless the implementing agency has the system to ensure the desired action against the defaulters, whenever they are infringed.

It is suggested that the security personnel should be deployed at the excavation sites from beginning till end for overall security management of the area. It is further suggested that the services of housekeeping staff and sweepers should be put under the control of security wing. Invariably, it has been noticed that the main entry and exit gates do not get proper attention and are not dusted and cleaned daily. Visitors must get the first impression right from the entry gate itself. Therefore, if the cleaning staffs render their services under the care of security wing then the cleaning of odd and neglected places could also be taken care of.

Security requires precise language and needs practical approach.

Management should keep morale of their staff high by taking care of 4Ps – Pay, Perks, Promotion and Postings.

The subject matter in this book is all about "Management of Heritage Sites from Security Point of View".

Continuous endeavour to upgrade security system by use of latest state-of-the-art technology and practices helps in matching the modus operandi of offenders.

APPENDIX I

IMPACT OF ENVIRONMENT ON MONUMENTS

Our century old rich and varied cultural heritage reflected through the monuments and sites are not only places of tourist interest but also the marvel of architectural excellence. Therefore, it is very important that they should be preserved at their best for the posterity.

Preservation and conservation of monuments is a very challenging task. It requires highly competent experts, since special technique and methodology are needed for this. Our country has varied climatic regions with environmental diversity. This affects the monuments. Besides, there are other factors like environmental pollution, which has adverse effect on them. Monuments in the marine area are susceptible to salt attack. Crystallization of these salts in dry atmosphere results in flaking off the surface of stone, thereby causing deterioration to the artefacts. Study has been carried out with Flame Photometer for determining the salt contents of different rock samples to estimate their extent of penetration in stone.

Experiments on the use of Epoxy-Resin for sealing the cracks in some of the monuments have been found to be quite satisfactory in preventing any penetration of water. Epoxy-Resin is neither susceptible to moisture nor does it shrink, thereby no question of physical damage to the monument. It has also been used for consolidation of crumbling stones.

Change in colour of marble of Taj Mahal, from white to yellowish attracted the attention of the concerned authorities and gave a reason for assessing the atmospheric conditions in and around Taj Mahal, Agra. Data of relative humidity, atmospheric temperature and stone surface temperature were undertaken, along with analysis of the specimen of the affected marbles.

Services of some agencies were outsourced in evaluating the pollutant levels in the air in the vicinity of Taj Mahal. A well-equipped laboratory is functioning at Agra to study the effect of air-pollution on Taj Mahal and other historical monuments. Automatic sulphur dioxide analyser is helping to keep a close eye over the level of sulphur dioxide in the vicinity of Taj and Sikandara. Air velocity, variation of temperature and humidity are recorded to study the factors, which may affect the stone monuments. Dust-fall studies are also being carried out in order to see the effect due to sedimentation of particulate matters. The efficacy of various preservatives over the marble to protect it against pollutants is also examined.

The matter of protecting the monuments from pollution is so important that a number of prime agencies like National Environmental Engineering Research Institute (NEERI), Nagpur; Ministry of Petroleum and Chemicals (Govt. of India), Indian Meteorological Department, National Aeronautical Laboratory, National Physical Research Laboratory, Raman Research Institute, Environmental Planning and Coordination Department of Science and Technology, Indian Institute of Petroleum, Indian Oil Corporation (IOC), Indian Railways (IR), Government of Uttar Pradesh and Archaeological Survey of India (ASI) etc. are actively involved.

Besides Taj some of the other important monuments which are getting due attention against environmental degradation are Jagannath Temple, Puri; Shore Temple at Mahabalipuram, Chennai; Elephanta, Mumbai etc. Efforts are on to protect Khajuraho archaeological site against vibrations due to Aircraft flying close over it.

APPENDIX II

DISASTERS

General

Disaster poses serious threat to the normal life as well as to the process of development. They strike with sudden violence, tearing bodies, destroying lives, families and structures apart. Natural disasters are both sudden and powerful. Human vulnerability to them is an age-old phenomenon. Monuments and artefacts are to be safeguarded in the event of various calamities and disasters. **Necessary equipments and special types of vehicles (Emergency Rescue Vehicles) may be requisition for dealing with the aftermath of disasters.**

Geological Disasters

(*a*) **Earthquake :** It is a sudden shift of the Earth's crust below or at the surface that results in ground vibration and the potential collapse of buildings and possible destruction of life and property, if the quake is of sufficient magnitude. Earthquakes are considered to be one of the most dangerous and disastrous natural phenomena. It is usually sudden with little or no warning. It is not yet possible to predict earthquakes and to make preparation against damages and collapses of buildings and other man made structures. An earthquake generates a set of horizontal and vertical vibrations of ground, which are random in character.

(*b*) **Tsunami :** It is popularly called tidal waves. 'Tsunami' is a Japanese word meaning "harbour wave". These are the waves which often affect distant shores, originate from undersea or coastal seismic activity, landslides and volcanic eruption. Whatever may be the cause, seawater is displaced into a violent motion and swells up, ultimately breaking over land with great destructive power. India too has faced major destruction due to Tsunami very recently. Its eastern coast and the Andaman & Nicobar Island suffered the brunt.

(*c*) **Volcanic Eruption :** Volcano is a vent or chimney to the earth's surface from a reservoir of molten rock, called magma, deep in the crust of earth. A study shows that approximately 600 volcanoes are active or have erupted. On an average, about 50 volcanoes erupt every year. At present, about 10% of world's population live on area near potentially dangerous volcanoes.

(*d*) **Landslides and Snow Avalanches :** Landslides generally occur as secondary effects of heavy storms, earthquakes and volcanic eruptions. It occurs as a result of changes, either sudden or gradual, in the composition, structure, hydrology or vegetation on a slope. Snow Avalanche is the rapid movement of large mass of snow, ice, earth, rock or other material in swift motion down a mountainside or over a precipice. Monuments located in mountainous terrain are vulnerable to these disasters.

Climatic Disasters

(*i*) **Cyclone :** It is a tropical storm in which the winds reach speeds over 120 kmph. Almost the entire East coast is vulnerable to cyclone with varying frequency and intensity. In the West coast, the North West coast (North of Mumbai) is more vulnerable as compared to South West coast (South of Mumbai). All the monuments located at the coastline are prone to adverse effects of cyclone and salt effect.

(*ii*) **Flood :** It can arise from abnormally heavy precipitation, dam failures, rapid snow melts, river blockages or even burst water mains.

Types of floods :

(*a*) Flash floods

(*b*) River floods

(*c*) Coastal floods

Typical Disasters

(*a*) **Forest Fire :** Forest fire constitute typical disaster phenomena the origins of which can be either natural or man-made. In their ferocity and destructive potential, these are notoriously dangerous. Fire spread rapidly and cause excessive damage to life and property, if not controlled in time. There are monuments which are situated within the forest area. They need to be taken care of the forest fire.

(*b*) **Building Fire :** This is the most common among the fire disasters. Unnecessary accumulation of combustible or inflammable articles or hazardous material adds to the danger. Lack of water or equipment for fire-fighting allows the fire to burn fiercely. Hot and dry seasons add to the possibility of fire as also the careless use of electrical equipment, improper wiring and loose joints. An electric short-circuit or a spark is often responsible for a large-scale fire disasters. The electric installations and wiring can cause fire in buildings when these get heated due to overload. People often do not realize that putting extra electrical load above the permissible limit causes overheating or break in the insulation in the electrical equipment which can either result in a spark or explosion or burn due to overheating. Museums, stores and offices need to be safeguarded accordingly.

(*c*) **Transportation Accidents :** The accidents in various modes of transport like roadways, airways, railways and seaways fall under this category. Therefore, these factors may be considered while moving the artefacts from one place to the other.

APPENDIX III

RELEVANT ACTS & RULES

(*a*) Ancient Monuments & Archaeological Sites and Remains Act, 1958 (24 of 1958).

(*b*) Ancient Monuments & Archaeological Sites and Remains Rules, 1959.

(*c*) Antiquities and Art Treasures Act, 1972.

(*d*) Antiquities and Art Treasures Rules, 1973.

(*e*) Contract Labour (Regulation and Abolition) Act, 1970 as amended in 2004 along with Rules, 1971.

(*f*) Prevention of Cruelty to Animals Act, 1960 and allied Rules.

(*g*) Private Security Agencies (Regulation) Act, 2005.

(*h*) Public Premises (Eviction of Unauthorised Occupants) Act, 1971 along with Rules, 1971.

(*i*) The Prevention of Damage to Public Property Act, 1984.

(*a*) ANCIENT MONUMENTS & ARCHAEOLOGICAL SITES AND REMAINS ACT, 1958 (24 of 1958)

There are two Acts relating to ancient monuments – The Ancient Monuments Preservation Act, 1904, and the Ancient and Historical Monuments and Archaeological Sites and Remains (Declaration of National Importance) Act, 1951. The Act of 1951 merely declares certain monuments, etc., to be of national importance and the Act of 1904 applies also to such monuments. While under the Constitution of India, the subject "Ancient and historical monuments; archaeological monuments; archaeological sites and remains", has been distributed under three heads, namely: Union List, Entry 67 – Ancient and historical monuments and records, and archaeological sites and remains declared by or under law made by Parliament to be of national importance; State list, Entry 12 – Ancient and historical monuments and records other than those declared by or under law made by Parliament to be of national importance; and concurrent List, Entry 40 – Archaeological sites and remains other than those declared by or under law made by Parliament to be of national importance. The Act of 1904 governs all ancient monuments whether falling in the Central field or the State field, and vests all executive powers in the Central Government. The then existing position relating to ancient monuments was found to be unsatisfactory, and the need was felt to legislate a self-contained law at the Centre which would apply exclusively to ancient monuments, etc., of national importance falling under Union List, Entry 67 and to archaeological sites and remains falling under Concurrent List, Entry 40. To achieve this objective the Ancient Monuments and Archaeological Sites and Remains Bill was introduced in the Parliament.

(*b*) ANCIENT MONUMENTS & ARCHAEOLOGICAL SITES AND REMAINS RULES, 1959

In exercise of the powers, conferred by section 38 of the Ancient Monuments and Archaeological Sites and Remains Act, 1958 (24 of 1958), the Central Government made the rules in 1959, which came into force on the 15th day of October, 1959. The rules extend to the whole of India, but rules 24, 25, 27, 28, 29 and 30 shall not apply to the State of Jammu and Kashmir.

(*c*) ANTIQUITIES AND ART TREASURES ACT, 1972

Antiquities (Export Control) Act, 1947 (31 of 1947) provided for controlling the export of objects of antiquarian or historical interest or significance. The provisions contained in the said Act were found to be not sufficient with a view to preserving objects of antiquity and art treasures in India. It was proposed to make comprehensive law to regulate the export trade in antiquities and art treasures and to provide for the prevention of smuggling of, and fraudulent dealings in antiquities. It was also considered necessary to make provisions in such law for the compulsory acquisition of antiquities and art treasures for preservation in public places and to provide for certain other matters connected therewith or incidental or ancillary thereto. To achieve the above objectives the Antiquities and Art Treasures Bill was introduced in the Parliament. The Antiquities and Art Treasures bill having been passed by both the Houses of Parliament received the assent of the President on 9th September, 1972. It came on Statute Book as THE ANTIQUITIES AND ART TREASURES ACT, 1972 (52 of 1972). This has undergone amendment and is known as The Antiquities and Art Treasures (Amendment) Act, 1976 (82 of 1976).

(*d*) ANTIQUITIES AND ART TREASURES RULES, 1973

In exercise of the powers conferred by section 31 of the Antiquities and Art Treasures Act, 1972 (52 of 1972), the Central Government made this rule. The Director General, Archaeological Survey of India shall be authority competent to issue permit under section 3 for the export of any antiquity or art treasure.

(*e*) CONTRACT LABOUR (REGULATION AND ABOLITION) ACT, 1970 AS AMENDED IN 2004 ALONGWITH CENTRAL RULES, 1971

The Contract Labour (Regulation and Abolition) Act, 1970 as its preamble suggests was brought on the statute book for two main objects : (1) to prohibit the employment of contract labour; and (2) to regulate the working conditions of the contract labour wherever such employment is not prohibited. The Contract Labour (Regulation and Abolition) Bill was passed by both the Houses of Parliament and subsequently received the assent of the President on 5th September, 1970 under the short title and the numbers THE CONTRACT LABOUR (REGULATION AND ABOLITION) ACT, 1970 (37 of 1970). It came into effect on 10th February, 1971. This has undergone amendments and is known as The Contract Labour (Regulation and Abolition) (Amendment) Act, 1986 (14 of 1986) and The Delegated Legislation Provisions (Amendment) Act, 2004 (4 of 2005). In exercise of the power conferred by section 35 of THE CONTRACT LABOUR (REGULATION AND ABOLITION) ACT, 1970 the Central Government made THE CONTRACT LABOUR (REGULATION AND ABOLITION) CENTRAL RULES, 1971 which came into force on 10.02.1971.

(*f*) PREVENTION OF CRUELTY TO ANIMALS ACT, 1960 AND ALLIED RULES

Animals are an integral part of Indian economy. Animals have been and are being used in various fields, specially agriculture, transportation and amusement, etc. To reap maximum gains human beings have exploited them by using coercive methods and by inflicting unnecessary pain. In order to prevent cruelty to animals the then British Government in India enacted the PREVENTION OF CRUELTY TO ANIMALS ACT, 1890 (11 of 1890). During the course of administering this Act many deficiencies were found. An Act was enacted to prevent the infliction of unnecessary pain or suffering on animals and for that purpose to amend the law relating to the prevention of cruelty to animals. The Bill having been passed by both the Houses of Parliament received the assent of the President on 26th December, 1960. It came on the Statute Book as THE PREVENTION OF CRUELTY TO ANIMALS ACT, 1960 (56 of 1960). This has undergone amendment and is known as THE PREVENTION OF CRUELTY TO ANIMALS (AMENDMENT) ACT, 1982 (26 of 1982).

(*g*) PRIVATE SECURITY AGENCIES (REGULATION) ACT, 2005

There has been tremendous growth in the number of private security agencies all over the country in recent years. In order to regulate the functioning of the private security agencies a bill namely "Private Security Agencies (Regulation) Bill" was introduced in the Parliament. The Rajya Sabha passed this bill on 10th May 2005 and the Lok Sabha on 12th May 2005 and received assent of the President on 23rd June 2005. It came on the Statute Book as "THE PRIVATE SECURITY AGENCIES (REGULATION) ACT, 2005 (29 of 2005)". The client while hiring the services of any private security agency must ensure the provisions contained in this Act. Relevant clauses of Labour Law and Act must also be taken care of.

(*h*) PUBLIC PREMISES (EVICTION OF UNAUTHORISED OCCUPANTS) ACT, 1971 ALONG WITH RULES, 1971

The Public Premises (Eviction of Unauthorised Occupants) Bill having been passed by both the Houses of Parliament received the assent of the

President on 23rd August, 1971. It came on Statute Book as "THE PUBLIC PREMISES (EVICTION OF UNAUTHORISED OCCUPANTS) ACT, 1971 (40 of 1971)". This has undergone amendments on several occasions and is known as The Public Premises (Eviction of Unauthorised Occupants) Amendment Act, 1980 (61 Of 1980); 1984 (35 of 1984) and 1993.

(*j*) THE PREVENTION OF DAMAGE TO PUBLIC PROPERTY ACT, 1984

In order to save public property by acts of vandalism, including destruction and damage caused during riots and public commotion, a need was felt to strengthen the law to enable the authorities to deal effectively with cases of damage to public property. Accordingly the President promulgated THE PREVENTION OF DAMAGE TO PUBLIC PROPERTY Ordinance on 28th January, 1984. To replace the said Ordinance by an Act of Parliament THE PREVENTION OF DAMAGE TO PUBLIC PROPERTY Bill was introduced in Parliament. This is known as THE PREVENTION OF DAMAGE TO PUBLIC PROPERTY ACT, 1984 (3 of 1984).

APPENDIX IV

NATIONAL MISSION ON MONUMENTS AND ANTIQUITIES

The Hon'ble Prime Minister of India launched the National Mission on Monuments and Antiquities on 19th March 2007. The National Mission on Monuments and Antiquities proposes to launch its activities throughout the country with independent functional strategy in each state and union territory. It is envisaged that mandate of the Mission would be achieved within a stipulated time frame of five years *i.e.,* 2007-12.

Built Heritage and Sites

According to the Ancient Monuments and Archaeological Sites and Remains Act, 1958 : **"Ancient Monuments"** means any structure, erection or monument, or any tumulus or place of interment, or any cave, rock sculpture, inscription or monolith, which is of historical, archaeological or artistic interest and which has been in existence for not less than hundred years and includes :

(*i*) Remains of an ancient monument,

(*ii*) Site of an ancient monument,

(*iii*) Such portion of land adjoining the site of an ancient monument as may be required for fencing or covering in or otherwise preserving such monument, and

(*iv*) The means of access to, and convenient inspection of an ancient monument.

However, for the purpose of documentation of Built Heritage under National Mission, the scope has been enhanced by defining any structure that belongs to pre-independence period, and 1950 has been considered as the cut off date. This has been decided realising the fact that heritage structure during pre-Independence period show the influence of colonial architecture and, sometimes, the traditional architecture of a region that is no more in continuity. Hence, these structures are unique to our present architectural tradition. Further, such built structures will be considered for documentation, which are architecturally, historically, archaeologically or aesthetically significant for reconstruction of regional history. The Built heritage and sites identified so far are only a fraction of the total wealth of the country. An even smaller figure is under the protection and care of the Central and State Governments. So far, only 3667 monuments and sites are protected by the Archaeological Survey of India (Feb., 2008) while approximately 3500 monuments and sites by the State Governments. Unfortunately, this unprotected heritage is fast disappearing at a pace, previously undreamt of, without any record because of the lack of public awareness on heritage and sustainable developmental projects.

Antiquity

According to the Antiquities and Art Treasures Act, 1972, "antiquity" includes,

I. (*i*) any coin, sculpture, painting, epigraph or other work of art or craftsmanship;

(*ii*) any article, object or thing detached from a building or cave;

(*iii*) any article, object or thing illustrative of science, art, crafts, literature, religion, customs, morals or politics in bygone ages;

(*iv*) any article, object or thing of historical interest;

(*v*) any article, object or thing declared by the Central Government, by notification in the Official Gazette, to be an antiquity for the purpose of this Act, which has been in existence for not less than one hundred years; and

II. any manuscript, record or other document which is of scientific, historical, literary or aesthetic value and which has been in existence for not less than seventy-five years.

Like built heritage and sites, India is rich in antiquarian wealth not only in quantity but also in its diversified varieties both in time and space. This vast wealth of antiquities is scattered all over and there is little or no information about them except for the antiquities that are either registered or kept in certain museums. In addition, the lack of public awareness and ignorance about the law are the reasons for an increasing trend of illicit trafficking of antiquities from India in the international market in recent years.

Mission Mandate

- ❑ Preparation of a National Register of Built Heritage, Sites and Antiquities.
- ❑ Setting up of State Level database on built heritage, sites and antiquarian wealth for information and dissemination to planners, researchers etc., and for better management of such cultural resources. It attempts to create a systematic, accessible and retrievable inventory of the built heritage, sites and antiquarian heritage of the country.
- ❑ Promoting awareness programmes regarding the benefits of preserving the historical and cultural aspects of built heritage, sites and antiquities.
- ❑ Extending training facility and capacity building to the concerned State departments, local bodies, NGOs, universities, museums, communities, etc. in the field of conservation of built heritage, and preservation and management of antiquarian remains.
- ❑ Developing synergy between institutions like ASI, State Departments, concerned institutions and NGOs to generate close interaction.

Activities

- ❑ Preparation of a National Register of Antiquities by documenting antiquities from primary and secondary sources.
- ❑ Preparation of a National Register of Built Heritage and Sites by compiling the existing records both published and unpublished.
- ❑ Preparation of a National Thematic Atlas of Built Heritage, Sites and Antiquities.
- ❑ Promoting awareness programmes about archaeological heritage and sensitising people about its preservation and management through various outreach programmes such as exhibitions, popular lectures,

advertisements through print and electronic media, etc.

- Sensitising people about documentation, preservation and preventive conservation of various types of antiquarian remains.
- Encouraging owners/institutions having built heritage to develop conservation management plans to preserve the integrity of their heritage buildings.
- Capacity building to the concerned State Departments, Local bodies, NGOs, universities, museums, communities, etc. in respect of heritage protection and preservation through training programmes, seminars and workshops.
- Publication of popular literature in various local languages for the people and educational institutions in respect of preservation and management of built heritage, sites and antiquities.
- Checking illicit trafficking of antiquities through public awareness and database on antiquities.
- Conservation of selected unprotected monuments.
- Help in formulating cultural policy at state and local levels.

APPENDIX V

WORLD HERITAGE MONUMENTS

In 1972, the General Conference of UNESCO adopted a resolution with overwhelming enthusiasm creating thereby a 'Convention concerning the protection of the World Cultural and Natural Heritage'. The main objectives of the convention were to define the World Heritage in both cultural and natural aspects, to enlist Sites and Monuments from the member countries which are of exceptional interest and universal value, the protection of which is the concern of all mankind; and to promote co-operation among all Nations and people to contribute for the protection of these universal treasures intact for future generations.

The recorded sites on the World Heritage list now stands little over 830 which includes both cultural and natural sites, and endowment that is shared by all mankind and the protection of which is our prime concern. India is an active member State on the World Heritage from 1977 and has been working in close co-operation with other International agencies like ICOMOS (International Council on Monuments and Sites), IUCN (International Union for the Conservation of Nature and Natural Resources) and ICCROM (International Centre for the Study of Preservation and Restoration of Cultural Property). The World Heritage has 22 Cultural and 5 Natural Sites from India. The Cultural Sites are Ajanta Caves; Ellora Caves; Agra Fort; Taj Mahal; Fatehpur Sikri, Agra; Sun Temple, Konark; Mahabalipuram Group of Monuments; Churches and Convents of Goa; Khajuraho Group of Monuments; Group of Monuments at Hampi; Group of Monuments at Pattadakal; Elephanta Caves; Brihadisvara Temple, Thanjavur with its extension including great living Chola temples Gangaikondacholisvaram and Airavatesvara at Darasuram; Buddhist Monuments at Sanchi; Humayun's Tomb, New Delhi; Qutb Complex, New Delhi; Red Fort, Delhi; Prehistoric

Rock Shelters of Bhimbetka; Champaner-Pavagadh Site – all under the Archaeological Survey of India besides Mountain Railways of India; Mahabodhi Temple, Bodh Gaya and Chhatrapati Shivaji Terminus (Formerly Victoria Terminus), Mumbai. The Natural Sites are Keoladeo National Park, Manas Wildlife Sanctuary, Kaziranga National Park, Sundarbans National Park and Nanda Devi National Park with its extension as Valley of Flowers.

The UNESCO has declared April 18 as the World Heritage Day and May 18 the World Museum Day. Apart from observing the World Heritage Day and augmenting various measures for conservation of the World Heritage Monuments, the Archaeological Survey of India has also decided to observe the World Heritage Week from 19th to 25th November every year. The World Heritage Week celebrations aim to involve the youth of the country through NSS (National Social Service) and NCC (National Cadet Corps) units in such works as protection, preservation and propagation of the great heritage for which our country is world famous.

(World Heritage Monuments Under the Archaeological Survey of India)

Sr. No.	*State*		*Location*		*Monument*
1.	Delhi		New Delhi	(i)	Humayun's Tomb
				(ii)	Red Fort
				(iii)	Qutb Minar Complex
2.	Goa		Velha Goa		Churches and Convents
3.	Gujarat		Champaner		Pavagadh Site
4.	Karnataka	(a)	Hampi	(i)	Group of Monuments
		(b)	Pattadakal	(ii)	Group of Monuments
5.	Kerala		Thanjavur		Group of Chola Temples
6.	Maharastra	(a)	Ajanta	(i)	Group of Caves
		(b)	Ellora	(ii)	Group of Caves
		(c)	Elephanta	(iii)	Group of Caves
7.	Madhya Pradesh	(a)	Khajuraho	(i)	Group of Monuments
		(b)	Sanchi	(ii)	Buddhist Monuments
		(c)	Bhimbetka	(iii)	Paintings in Rock Shelters
8.	Orissa		Konark		Sun Temple
9.	Tamil Nadu		Mahabalipuram		Group of Monuments
10.	Uttar Pradesh		Agra	(i)	Taj Mahal
				(ii)	Agra Fort
				(iii)	Fatehpur Sikri

(Not Under The Archaeological Survey of India)

Sr. No.	*State*	*Location*	*Monument*
1.	Bihar	Bodh Gaya	Mahabodhi Temple
2.	West Bengal	Darjeeling	Mountain Railways
3.	Maharastra	Mumbai	Chhatrapati Shivaji Terminus

Every site, monument and museum is different in nature from security angle.

APPENDIX VI

MUSEUMS

National Museum and Others of Same Status

Sr. No.	State	Location	Monument
1.	Delhi	Janpath	National Museum
2.	Andhra Pradesh	Hyderabad	Salarjung Museum
3.	Maharastra	Mumbai	Prince of Wales Museum
4.	Uttar Pradesh	Allahabad	Allahabad Museum
5.	West Bengal	Kolkata	Indian Museum

Site Museums Under A.S.I.

Sr.No.	State	Location	Monument
1.	Andhra Pradesh	Amaravati, District Guntur	1. Archaeological Museum, Amaravati
		Chandragiri, District Chittoor	2. Archaeological Museum, Chandragiri
		Kondapur, District Medak	3. Archaeological Museum, Kondapur
		Nagarjunakonda, District Guntur	4. Archaeological Museum, Nagarjunakonda
2.	Assam	Sri Surya Pahar, District Goalpara	5. Archaeological Museum, Sri Surya Pahar
3.	Bihar	Antichak, District Bhagalpur	6. Archaeological Museum, Vikramshila
		Bodh Gaya, District Gaya	7. Archaeological Museum, Bodh Gaya
		Nalanda, District Nalanda	8. Archaeological Museum, Nalanda
		Vaishali, District Vaishali	9. Archaeological Museum, Vaishali
4.	Delhi	Red Fort, Delhi	10. Archaeological Museum, Red Fort
		Red Fort, Delhi	11. Indian War Memorial Museum, Red Fort
		Purana Qila, Delhi	12. Archaeological Museum, Purana Qila
		Red Fort, Delhi	13. Swatantrata Sangram Sanghrahalaya, Red Fort
		Red Fort, Delhi	14. Archaeological Museum, Salimgarh
5.	Gujarat	Lothal, District Ahmedabad	15. Archaeological Museum, Lothal
		Dholavira, District Bhuj	16. Archaeological Museum, Dholavira
6.	Goa	Velha Goa, North Goa	17. Archaeological Museum, Velha Goa
7.	Haryana	Thaneswar, District Kurukshetra	18. Archaeological Museum, Sheikh Chili's Tomb
8.	Himachal Pradesh	Kangra, District Kangra	19. Archaeological Museum, Kangra Fort

Sr.No.	*State*	*Location*	*Monument*
9.	Karnataka	Aihole, District Bagalkot	20. Archaeological Museum, Aihole
		Bijapur, District Bijapur	21. Archaeological Museum, Bijapur
		Badami, District Bagalkot	22. Archaeological Museum, Badami
		Halebidu, District Hassan	23. Archaeological Museum, Haleibidu
		Kamalapur, District Bellary	24. Archaeological Museum, Hampi
		Daria Daulta Bagh, Sringapattana, District Mandya	25. Archaeological Museum, Tipu Sultan Palace
10.	Kerala	Ernakulam, District Kochi	26. Archaeological Museum, Mattanchery Palace
11.	Madhya Pradesh	Sanchi, District Raisen	27. Archaeological Museum, Sanchi
		Chanderi, District Ashok Nagar	28. Archaeological Museum, Singhpur Palace, Chanderi
		Gwalior, District Gwalior	29. Archaeological Museum, Gwalior Fort
		Khajuraho, District Chhatarpur	30. Archaeological Museum, Khajuraho
12.	Orissa	Konark, District Puri	31. Archaeological Museum, Konark
		Ratnagiri, District Jajpur	32. Archaeological Museum, Ratnagiri
13.	Punjab	Rupnagar, District Rupnagar	33. Archaeological Museum, Ropar
14.	Rajasthan	Kalibangan, District Hanumangarh	34. Archaeological Museum, Kalibangan
15.	Tamil Nadu	Fort St. George, Chennai	35. Archaeological Museum, Fort St. George
16.	Uttar Pradesh	Sarnath, District Varanasi	36. Archaeological Museum, Sarnath
		Residency, Lucknow	37. Archaeological Museum, Residency, Lucknow
		Agra, District Agra	38. Archaeological Museum, Taj Mahal
17.	Uttarakhand	Jageshwar, District Almora,	39. Archaeological Museum. Jageshwar
18.	West Bengal	Murshidabad, District Murshidabad	40. Hazarduari Palace Museum, Murshidabad
		Koch Behar, District Koch Behar	41. Archaeological Museum, Koch Behar Palace
		Tamluk, District Purba Medinapur	42. Archaeological Museum, Tamluk

APPENDIX VII

UNIFORM ITEMS (Male & Female)

1. Shirt & trousers, Salwar-kurta or, Sari-blouse
2. Cap
3. Belt
4. Identity card
5. Socks
6. Shoes (Gents and Ladies)
7. Chappal/Sandal (Gents and Ladies)
8. Lanyard
9. Nameplate
10. Badges (for cap, shoulders and belt)
11. Medals and ribbons (as applicable)
12. Gumboot
13. Umbrella
14. Raincoat
15. Woollen jersey
16. Woollen shortcoat/overcoat
17. Bulletproof jacket (need based)
18. Helmet (need based)

APPENDIX VIII

SECURITY ITEMS AND PROVISIONS

1. Baton
2. Long stick
3. Small arms – at identified duty points
4. Whistle
5. Walkie-talkie
6. High beam torch
7. Key chain
8. Knife
9. Water bottle
10. SITREP form
11. Pen
12. Lantern
13. Binocular – at identified duty points
14. Night vision device – for exclusively identified duty points
15. Bulletproof jacket – at identified duty points
16. Helmet
17. Shield
18. Siren
19. Public address system
20. Stop barriers – at entry and exit points as well as at other identified points

21. Sentry posts
22. Bullet proof sentry posts (morcha) – at identified duty points
23. Sign posts
24. Hand-held metal detectors
25. Doorframe metal detectors
26. Burglar alarm
27. CCTV (Close Circuit Television)
28. Trained dogs
29. Security lights
30. Electricity back-up system (Generator set, solar power system etc.)
31. Transport (two wheeler, car, jeep, van and truck etc.)

APPENDIX IX

FIRE-FIGHTING EQUIPMENTS AND PROVISIONS

1. Fire extinguisher (different types and capacity)
2. Fire bucket
3. Fire beater
4. Stretcher
5. Blanket
6. First-aid box
7. Telephone numbers of fire station, police station, nearest nursing home and hospitals should be displayed at conspicuous places.
8. Fire points having all the provisions.
9. Fire Sensors
10. Smoke Detectors
11. Fire Alarms
12. Telescopic Ladder

APPENDIX X

FIRST-AID NECESSITIES

1. First-Aid box
2. Savalon Liquid
3. Dettol
4. Cotton
5. Bandage
6. Band Aid
7. Micro Tape
8. Betadine Cream
9. Soframicine Cream
10. Burnol Cream
11. Crocin Analgesic Tablets
12. Combiflam Tablets
13. ORS Powder
14. Doctor's Knife
15. Doctor's Scissors

MONUMENTS AND SITES OF INDIA INSCRIBED ON WORLD HERITAGE LIST OF UNESCO

BUDDHIST MONUMENT AT SANCHI (1989)

Imposing Stupa 1 with four gateways and railings made Sanchi a world famous Buddhist site. The original stupa of the Asokan times was enlarged and faced with stones. It is decorated with balustrades, staircases and an umbrella on top. Besides this, other stupas, monolithic Asokan pillar, many other temples, monasteries and sculptures are found scattered at Sanchi and its adjoining hills from the Mauryan period to the twelfth century AD.

In the first century BC, the Andhra-Satavahanas extended their sway over the eastern Malwa and carved the elaborate gateways to Stupa 1 with the stories of the life of Buddha who was worshipped here in symbolic form. The inscriptions on the gateways and railings record the donation made by the corporate guilds and individuals.

From the second to the fourth century AD, Sanchi along with Vidisa came under the Kushan and Kshatrapa rulers and subsequently passed on to the hands of the Guptas when some temples were built and decorated with sculptures. Some shrines and monasteries were also constructed during the seventh to the twelfth century AD (Plate 1).

AJANTA CAVES (1983)

The world famous Ajanta Caves including the unfinished ones are thirty in number, of which five (9, 10, 19, 26, and 29) are *chaitya-grihas* and rest *viharas* (monasteries). After centuries of oblivion, these caves were discovered in AD 1819. They fall into two distinct phases with a break of nearly four centuries between them. All the caves of the earlier phase date between second century BC-AD. The caves of the second phase were excavated during the supremacy of the Vakatakas and Guptas.

A few paintings, which survive on the walls of Caves 9 and 10 date back to the second century BC-AD. The second group of the paintings started in about the fifth century AD and continued for the next two centuries as noticeable in later Caves. Caves 1, 2, 16 and 17 have remarkable paintings with themes intensely religious in tone and centre around Buddha, Bodhisattvas, incidents from the life of Buddha and the *jatakas.* The paintings are executed on a ground of mud-plaster in the tempera technique (Plate 2).

ELLORA CAVES (1983)

The magnificent group of rock-cut shrines of Ellora, representing three different faiths, Buddhist, Brahmanical and Jaina were excavated during the period from fifth to the thirteenth century AD. The Buddhist Caves (1 to 12) were excavated between the fifth and the seventh centuries AD, when the Mahayana sects were flourishing in the region. Important in this group are Caves 5, 10 and 12.

The Brahmanical Caves numbering 13 to 29 are mostly Saivite. Kailasa (Cave 16) is a remarkable example of rock-cut temples in India on account of its striking proportion, elaborate workmanship, architectural content and sculptural ornamentation. There are two *dhvaja-stambhas* or pillars with flagstaff in the courtyard. The grand sculpture of Ravana attempting to lift mount Kailasa, the abode of Siva, with his full might is a landmark in Indian art.

The Jaina Caves (30 to 34) are massive, well-proportioned, decorated and mark the last phase of the activity at Ellora (Plate 3).

ELEPHANTA CAVES (1987)

Elephanta anciently known as Gharapuri, the island capital of Konkan Mauryas, is celebrated for its colossal image of Mahesamurti with three heads each representing a different form.

In fact, there are seven caves out of which the most important is the Mahesa-murti cave. The main body of the cave, excluding the porticos on the three open sides and the back isle is 27 metres square and is supported by rows of six columns each. The gigantic figures of *dvarapalas* or doorkeepers here are very impressive.

There are sculptured compartments in this cave with remarkable images of Ardhanarisvara, Kalyana-Sundara Siva, Ravana lifting Kailasa, Andhakari-murti (slaying of Andhaka demon) and Nataraja Siva (Plate 4).

MAHABALIPURAM GROUP OF MONUMENTS (1984)

Mahabalipuram or Mamallapuram, the city of Mamalla, is named after the title of great Pallava ruler Narasimhavarman-l (AD 630-668). It was a sea-port during the time of *periplus* (first century AD) and Ptolemy (AD 140) and many India colonists sailed to South-East Asia through this port town. While there is some evidence of architectural activity going back to the period of Mahendravarman-l (AD 600-630), the father of Mamalla, most of the monuments like rock-cut *rathas*, sculptured scenes on open rocks like Arjuna's penance, the caves of Govardhanadhari and Mahishasuramardini, the Jala-Sayana Perumal temple (the sleeping Mahavishnu or Chakrin at the rear part of the Shore temple complex) are attributed to the period of Narasimhavarman-l Mamalla.

The monolithic Dharmaraja, Arjun and Draupadi *rathas* are square on plan, the Bhima and Ganesa *rathas* are rectangular and Sahadeva *ratha* apsidal. Though monolithic sculpturing, both cut- in and cut-out, continued even during later periods (Atiranachanda cave, Pidari *rathas* and Tiger-cave). The structural architecture was introduced on a grand scale by Pallava Rajasimha (AD 700-728), culminating in erection of the world famous Shore temple. The later period witnessed a few additions during the late-Pallava and Chola times. The grandiose Vijayanagara phase here is represented by the Raja Gopurams and the Sthala-Sayana temple, juxtaposed to the carved boulder of Arjuna's penance (Plate 5).

PATTADAKAL GROUP OF MONUMENTS (1987)

Pattadakal is not only popular for Chalukyan architecture but it is also a holy place for royal coronation, Pattadaksuvolal. Temples constructed here mark the blending of the Rekha-Nagara-Prasada and the Dravida Vimana styles of temple building.

The oldest temple at Pattadakal is Sangamesvara built by Vijayaditya Satyasraya (AD 697-733). It is a simple but massive structure.

Virupaksha temple of the Chalukyan period served as a model for the Rashtrakuta ruler to carve out the great Kailasa at Ellora. The sculptural art of the early Chalukyas is characterised by grace and delicate details, the ceiling panels of the *navagrahas dikpalas,* the dancing Nataraja, the wall niches containing Lingodbhava, Ardhanarisvara, Tripurari, Varahavishnu, Trivikrama bear ample testimony to the sculptor's skill as well as the cult worship in vogue. The narrative reliefs illustrating certain episodes from the *Ramayana, Mahabharata, Bhagavata* and *Panchatantra* fitted well with these grand religious edifices (Plate 6).

KHAJURAHO GROUP OF MONUMENTS (1986)

Khajuraho, the ancient Kharjjuravahaka, was the principal seat of authority of the Chandella rulers who adorned it with numerous tanks, scores of lofty temples of sculptural grace and architectural splendor. The local tradition lists eighty- five temples but now only twenty-five are standing examples in various stages of preservation. But for Chausath-Yogini, Brahma and Mahadeva which are of granite, all the other temples are of fine grained sandstone, buff, pink or pale yellow in colour. The Lakshmana temple dedicated to Vishnu built by Yasovarman (AS 954), is an ornate and evolved example.

The Visvanatha, Parsvanatha and Vaidyanatha temples belong to the time of king Dhanga, the successor of Yasovarman. The Jagadambi and Chitragupta are noteworthy among the western group of temples. The largest and grandest temple of Khajuraho is the immortal Kandariya Mahadeva which is attributed to king Ganda (AD 1017-1029). The other examples that followed *viz.,* Vamana, Adinatha, Javari, Chaturbhuj and Duladeo, are smaller but elaborately designed. The Khajuraho group of temples are noted for lofty terraces (jagati) and functionally effective plans. The sculptures of divine and semi-divine being win universal admiration for their delicate modelling. Youthful female forms with their ravishing attire and ornaments also embrace the winsome grace and charm (Plate 7).

THE GREAT LIVING CHOLA TEMPLES (1987)

The celebrated Saiva temple, appropriately called *Brihadisvara* and *Dakshinameru*, is the grandest creation of the Chola emperor Rajaraja (AD 985-1012) at Thanjavur. It was inaugurated by the king himself in his 19th regnal year and named it after himself as Rajesvara Peruvudaiyar. Architecturally, it is the most ambitious structural temple built of granite. The temple is within a spacious inner *prakara* of 240.90 m long (east-west) and 122 m broad (north-south), with a *gopura* at the east and three other ordinary *torana* entrances one at each lateral sides and the third at rear.

The *sikhara*, a cupolic dome, is octagonal and rests on a single block of granite, a square of 7.8 m weighing 80 tons. The majestic *upapitha* and *adhishthana* are common to all the axially placed entities like the *ardha*, *maha* and *mukha-mandapas* and linked to the main sanctum but approached through a north-south transept across the *ardha-mandapa* which is marked by lofty *sopanas*. The moulded plinth is extensively engraved with inscriptions by its royal builder who refers to his many endowments, pious acts and organisational events connected to the temple. The *brihad-linga* within the sanctum is 8.7 m high. Life-size iconographic representations on the wall niches and inner passages include Durga, Lakshmi, Sarasvati and Bhikshatana, Virabhadra, Kalantaka, Natesa, Ardhanarisvara and Alingana forms of Siva. The mural paintings on the walls of the lower ambulatory inside are finest examples of Chola and later periods.

As an extension to the Brihadisvara temple of Thanjavur which was inscribed as World Heritage site in 1987, two more Chola temples have been added to it. The site now includes the three great eleventh and twelfth century Chola Temples, *i.e.,* the Brihadisvara temple of Thanjavur, the temple of Gangaikondacholisvaram and the Airavatesvara temple at Darasuram.

The temple of Gangaikondacholisvaram, built by Rajendra I with its 53 m vimana (sanctum tower) has recessed corners and a graceful upward curving movement, contrasting with the straight and severe tower at

Thanjavur. It has massive, monolithic dvarapala statues guarding the entrances.

The Airavatesvara temple complex, built by Rajaraja II, at Darasuram features a 24 m vimana and a stone image of Siva. The three Chola temples of Southern India collectively represent an outstanding creative achievement in the architectural conception of the pure from of the Dravida type of temple, sculpture and painting (Plates 8*a*, 8*b* & 8*c*).

SUN TEMPLE AT KONARK (1984)

Konark is the Kainapara of the *periplus* (first century AD)–an important port of the Orissan coast. The most notable marvel is the stately Sun Temple, built in *c.*AD 1250, during the reign of the Eastern Ganga King Narasimhadeva-I (AD 1238-1264), to enshrine an image of Sun (*Arka*) the patron deity of the place. The entire complex was designed in the form of a huge chariot drawn by seven spirited horses on twelve pairs of exquisitely carved wheels. The sanctum symbolises the majestic stride of the Sun-God and marks the culmination of the Orissan architectural style. The walls of the temple contain superb carvings of divine, semi-divine, human and animal figures amidst floral and geometric ornamentations. The vivacious *kanyas*, dancers and musicians are remarkable for their sensuous modelling, pulsating with human emotions which are absorbed in a variety of gestures and rhythmic action. Mighty *simha-gajas* welcome the visitor at the porches (Plate 9).

QUTB COMPLEX, DELHI (1993)

Qutb Minar in red and buff sandstone is the highest tower in India. It has a diameter of 14.32m at the base and about 2.75m on the top with a height of 72.5m.

Qutbu'd-Din Aibak laid the foundation of Minar in AD 1199 for the use of the mu'azzin (crier) to give calls for prayer and raised the first storey, to which were added three more storeys by his successor and son-in-law, Shamsu'd Din Iltutmish (AD 1211-1236). All the storeys are surrounded by a projected balcony encircling the minar and supported by stone brackets, which are decorated with honey-comb design, more conspicuously in the first storey.

Numerous inscriptions in Arabic and Nagari characters in different places of the minar reveal the history of Qutb. According to the inscriptions on its surface it was repaired by Firuz Shah Tughlaq (AD 1351-1388) and Sikandar Lodi (AD 1489-1517).

Quwwat-ul-Islam Mosque, to the north-east of minar was built by Qutbu'd-Din Aibak in AD 1198. It is the earliest extant mosque built by the Delhi Sultans. It consists of a rectangular courtyard enclosed by cloisters, erected with the carved columns and architectural members of 27 Hindu and Jaina temples as recorded in the inscription on the main eastern entrance. Later, a lofty arched screen was erected and the mosque was enlarged by Shamsu'd-Din Iltutmish and Alau'd-din Khalji. The Iron pillar in the courtyard bears an inscription in Sanskrit in Brahmi script of fourth century AD, according to which the pillar was set up as a Vishnudhvaja (standard of God Vishnu) on the hill known as Vishnupada in memory of a mighty king named Chandra. A deep socket on the top of the ornate capital indicates that probably an image of Garuda was fixed into it.

The tomb of Iltutmish was built in AD 1235. It is a plain square chamber of red sandstone, profusely carved with inscriptions, geometrical and arabesque patterns in Saracenic tradition on the entrances and the whole of interior.

Ala'i-Darwaza, the southern gateway of the Quwwat-ul-Islam Mosque was constructed by Alu'd-Din Khalji in AH 710 (AD 1311) as recorded in the inscriptions engraved on it.

Ala'i Minar which stands to the north of Qutb Minar, was commenced by Alau'd-Din Khalji, with the intention of making it twice the size of earlier Minar. He could complete only the first storey which now has an extant height of 25m. (Plate 10).

HAMPI GROUP OF MONUMENTS (1986)

Hampi, on the southern bank of the Tungabhadra, once formed the seat of mighty Vijayanagara empire. The contemporary chroniclers who came from far off countries like Arabia, Italy, Portugal and Russia visited the empire and have left graphic and glowing accounts of the city. Monuments were built here between AD 1336 and 1570, from the time of Harihara I to that of Sadasiva Raya. Royal buildings were raised by Krishnadeva Raya (AD 1509-1530). Hampi covers an area of nearly 26 sq. km and is enclosed by seven lines of fortifications. Within the innermost enclosure extensive remains of the palace are noticed. Temples of this city are noted for their large dimensions, florid ornamentation, bold and delicate carvings, stately pillars, magnificent pavilions and sculptural depictions from the Ramayana and the Mahabharata.

The largest extant temple is that of Pampapati with magnificent entrance tower caused by Krishnadeva Raya. The Vitthala temple is an excellent example of Vijayanagara style. The monolithic statues of Lakshmi, Narasimha and Ganesa are massive and graceful. The Krishna temple, Pattabhirama temple, Hazara Ramachandra, Chandrasekhara temple and the Jaina temples are noteworthy. Some temples are flanked on either side by storeyed mandapas. The audience hall of the king, Zenana enclosure with a massive stone basement of the Queen's palace and an ornate pavilion 'Lotus Mahal' are examples of secular architecture. The corner towers, Dhananyaka's enclosure (treasury), Mahanavami Dibba with sculptured panels, a variety of ponds, tanks, mandapas, elephant stables, pillared mandapas are awe-inspiring (Plate 11).

ROCK SHELTERS OF BHIMBETKA (2003)

The Rock Shelters of Bhimbetka are in the foothills of the Vindhyan Mountains on the southern edge of the Central Indian plateau. Within massive sandstone outcrops, above comparatively dense forest, are five clusters of natural rock shelters, displaying paintings that appear to date from the Mesolithic Period right through the historical period. Excavations from time to time have shown that the site had a continuous cultural remains from Palaeolithic to historic period.

The site of Bhimbetka spread over 10 km in length has more than 700 rock shelters, of which over 400 have paintings. The natural setting with geological formations with which the human culture was associated is noteworthy. Bhimbetka reflects a long interaction between people and the landscape, as demonstrated in the quantity and quality of its rock art. It also got the evidence of living tradition in the form of art among the aboriginals of the area.

The continuity of human settlement from the Lower Palaeolithic to Upper Palaeolithic period is exhibited by array of stone tools with characteristic features. Bhimbetka witnessed a drastic change in the Mesolithic Period in tool typology and raw material.

Though Bhimbetka is known for prehistoric remains, evidence of Buddhist structures in the form of small stupas have also been discovered. Some of the caves also bear inscriptions datable to Maurya and Sunga period (Plate 12*a* & *b*).

CHAMPANER-PAVAGADH SITE (2004)

The impressive archaeological remains, located about fifty kms from Baroda (Gujarat) are at the foot of the Pavagadh hill. It was a prosperous medieval capital which ranked with other medieval capitals *viz.,* Fatehpur Sikri and Vijayanagara.

The spectacular Pavagadh hill contains some of the old rock formations of India. Champaner, with impressive natural setting, encompasses vestiges of prehistoric times, a hill fortress of early Hindu capital and remains of the fifteenth century deserted medieval capital. A temple atop the hill is dedicated to Kalikamata.

Khichi Chauhans conquered the city in the tenth century and the area remained under their control till AD 1484. The oldest existing monuments including temples, fortification and extensive water storage systems belong to this period. After Muslim intervention Champaner was annexed by Musafarids of Gujarat in AD 1484. During this phase the settlement was shifted to the foot of the hill and cradled the deserted capital established by Mahmud Begharda interspersed with tanks, waterways, walls, bastions and remnants of medieval military architecture.

The site, in total, offers a variety of built heritage components like armoury, barracks, catapults, gates, fortifications, pavilions, religious structures both temples and mosques, civic structures like stepped-wells, water-storage system, bridge, roads, residential and commercial precincts. The Jama Masjid and Nagina Masjid are some of the outstanding examples to represent Gujarat regional style of architecture (Plate 13).

MUGHAL CITY AT FATEHPUR SIKRI (1986)

In honour of saint Shaikh Salim Chishti, the Mughal emperor Akbar the great, founded a magnificent city on Sikri ridge. In 1571 he ordered the construction of buildings for his own use and asked the noblemen to build houses for themselves. Within a year, most of the work was finished and within the next few years, a well planned city with administrative, residential and religious buildings came into existence.

The Jami Mosque was perhaps among the first buildings to come up. Its epigraph provides AH 979 (AD 1571-1572) as the date of its completion. The Buland-Darwaza was added some five years later.

Among other important buildings are the tomb of Shaikh Salim Chishti, the Naubat-or-Naqqar Khana (drum-house), Taksal (mint), Karkhanas (royal workshops), Khazana (treasury), Hakim's Quarters, Diwan-i-Am (hall of public audience), house of Maryam also called Sunahra Makan (Golden House), palace of Jodha Bai, Birbal's house etc. (Plate 14).

CHURCHES AND CONVENTS OF GOA (1986)

Velha Goa (Goa) is famous for the most spectacular group of churches and cathedrals built during the sixteenth and seventeenth centuries AD. These includes Se'Cathedral, Church and Convent of St. Francis of Assisi, Chapel of St. Catherine, Basilica of Bom Jesus, Church of the Lady of Rosary and Church of St. Augustine. The Church of St. Cajetan is modelled on the original design of St. Peter's Church in Rome. The Church of Bom Jesus with its facade is decorated with Ionic, Doric and Corinthian pilasters.

The paintings in the churches were done on wooden borders and fixed between panels having floral designs as in the chapels housing the tomb of St. Xavier, the arches above the altars in the transept of the Se' Cathedral and in the nave on either side of the main altar in the Church of St. Francis of Assisi. There are delicately carved painted wooden statues besides a few in stone to adorn the altars, depicting mostly the saints, Mother Mary and Jesus on the cross (Plates 15*a* & 15*b*).

HUMAYUN'S TOMB, DELHI (1993)

The first substantial example of a garden tomb on *charbagh* pattern with high arches and double dome was erected by Humayun's queen Hamida Banu Begam (Haji Begam) in AD 1569 at a cost of 15 lakh rupees (1.5 million).

The high rubble built enclosure is entered through two lofty double-storeyed gateways on the west and south. A *baradari* (pavilion) occupies the center of the eastern wall and a *hammam* (bath chamber) in the center of northern wall. The lofty mausoleum is in the center of the enclosure and rises from a podium faced with a series of cells having arched openings. Red sandstone and marble have been used for veneering. The central octagonal chamber contains the cenotaph, encompassed by octagonal chambers at the diagonals and arched lobbies on the sides. Their openings are closed with perforated screens. Each side is dominated by three arches, the central one being the highest. This plan is repeated on the second storey also. The roof surmounted by a double dome (42.5m) of marble has pillared kiosks (*chhatris*) placed around it.

Several rulers of the Mughal dynasty lie buried here. Bahadur Shah Zafar had taken refuge in this tomb with three princes during the first war of Independence (AD 1857).

On the southwestern side of the tomb is located Barber's tomb (Nai-Ka-Gumbad) which stands on a raised platform, reached by seven steps from the south. The building is square on plan and consists of a single compartment covered with a double-dome (Plate 16).

AGRA FORT (1983)

Agra Fort represents the first major building project of Akbar, with remains of only a few buildings built by him which now survive. Built on the site of an earlier castle in AD 1565-1575, the fort, apart from other important units, contains Jahangiri Mahal, Khass Mahal, Diwan-i-Khass, Diwan-i-Am, Machchhi Bhawan and Moti Masjid. Many extant buildings were erected by Shah Jahan (AD 1630-1655). Of its four gates, the most impressive is the Delhi Gate on the west (Plate 17).

TAJ MAHAL (1983)

Taj on the right bank of River Yamuna, about 1.5 km from the Agra fort, was built to enshrine the remains of Arjumand Banu Begam entitled Mumtaj Mahal, the queen of the Mughal emperor Shah Jahan. Its construction commenced in AD 1631 and completed seventeen years later at an enormous cost and labour. The intricate carvings and inlay work in marble enhance the beauty of Taj in which the emperor was also buried by the side of his queen after his death. Unlike other Mughal garden tombs, the mausoleum is situated at the northern end of a large rectangular area with its central portion divided into a square garden. The Taj is entered through a majestic gateway in the centre of the southern side where there is a spacious quadrangle. The monument is considered to be an epitome of love and one of the most flawless architectural creations of the world (Plate 18).

RED FORT COMPLEX (2007)

The Red Fort Complex was built as the palace fort of Shahjahanabad–the new capital of the fifth Mughal Emperor of India, Shah Jahan. Named for its massive enclosing walls of red sandstone, it is adjacent to an older fort, the Salimgarh, built by Islam Shah Sur in 1546, with which it forms the Red Fort Complex. The private apartments consist of a row of pavilions connected by a continuous water channel, known as the Nahr-i-Behisht (Stream of Paradise). The Red Fort is considered to represent the zenith of Mughal creativity which, under the Shah Jahan, was brought to a new level of refinement. The planning of the palace is based on Islamic prototypes, but each pavilion reveals architectural elements typical of Mughal building, reflecting a fusion of Persian, Timurid and Hindu traditions. The Red Fort's innovative planning and architectural style, including the garden design, strongly influenced later buildings and gardens in Rajasthan, Delhi, Agra and further afield (Plate 19).

MAHABODHI TEMPLE COMPLEX, BODH GAYA (2002)

The Mahabodhi Temple Complex is one of the four holy sites related to the life of Lord Buddha, and particularly to the attainment of Enlightenment. The first temple was built by Emperor Asoka in the 3rd century B.C., and the present temple dates from the 5th or 6th centuries. It is one of the earliest Buddhist temples built entirely in brick, still standing in India, from the late Gupta period (Plate 20).

Justification for Inscription

Criterion (i) : The grand 50 m high Mahabodhi Temple of the 5th-6th centuries is of immense importance, being one of the earliest temple constructions existing in the Indian sub-continent. It is one of the few representations of the architectural genius of the Indian people in constructing fully developed brick temples in that era.

Criterion (ii) : The Mahabodhi Temple, one of the few surviving examples of early brick structures in India, has had significant influence in the development of architecture over the centuries.

Criterion (iii) : The site of the Mahabodhi Temple provides exceptional records for the events associated with the life of Buddha and subsequent worship, particularly since Emperor Asoka built the first temple, the balustrades, and the memorial column.

Criterion (iv) : The present Temple is one of the earliest and most imposing structures built entirely in brick from the late Gupta period. The sculpted stone balustrades are an outstanding early example of sculptural relief in stone.

Criterion (v) : The Mahabodhi Temple Complex in Bodh Gaya has direct association with the life of the Lord Buddha, being the place where He attained the supreme and perfect insight.

CHHATRAPATI SHIVAJI TERMINUS (2004)
(Formerly Victoria Terminus)

The Chhatrapati Shivaji Terminus, formerly known as Victoria Terminus Station, in Mumbai (Bombay), is an outstanding example of Victorian Gothic Revival architecture in India, blended with themes deriving from Indian traditional architecture. The building, designed by the British architect F.W. Stevens, became the symbol of Bombay as the 'Gothic City' and the major international mercantile port of India. The terminal was built over 10 years, starting in 1878, according to a High Victorian Gothic design based on late medieval Italian models. Its remarkable stone dome, turrets, pointed arches and eccentric ground plan are close to traditional Indian palace architecture. It is an outstanding example of the meeting of two cultures, as British architects worked with Indian craftsmen to include Indian architectural tradition and idioms thus forging a new style unique to Bombay (Plate 21).

Justification for Inscription in UNESCO list

Criterion (*ii*) : Chhatrapati Shivaji Terminus of Mumbai (formerly Bombay) exhibits an important interchange of influences from Victorian Italianate Gothic Revival architecture, and from Indian traditional buildings. It became a symbol for Mumbai as a major mercantile port city on the Indian Subcontinent within the British Commonwealth.

Criterion (*iv*) : Chhatrapati Shivaji Terminus is an outstanding example of late 19th century railway architecture in the British Commonwealth, characterized by Victorian Gothic Revival and traditional Indian features, as well as its advanced structural and technical solutions.

MOUNTAIN RAILWAYS OF INDIA (1999 & 2005)

The site includes the Darjeeling Himalayan Railway, inscribed in UNESCO list in 1999. The site now encompasses the Nilgiri Mountain Railway, a 46 km long metre-gauge single-track railway in Tamil Nadu State. Its construction was first proposed in 1854, but due to the difficulty of the mountainous location the work only started in 1891 and was completed in 1908. This railway, scaling an elevation of 326 m to 2,203 m and still in use today, represented the latest technology of the time. It was significant in facilitating population movement and socio-economic development in the British colonial era (Plate 22).

Justification for Inscription in UNESCO list

Criterion (ii): The mountain railways of India are outstanding examples of the interchange of values on developments in technology, and the impact of innovative transportation system on the social and economic development of a multicultural region, which was to serve as a model for similar developments in many parts of the world.

Criterion (iv) : The development of railways in the 19th century had a profound influence on social and economic developments in many parts of the world. The Mountain Railways of India are outstanding examples of a technological ensemble, representing different phases of the development in high mountain areas.

Notes

The "Darjeeling Himalayan Railway" which was previously inscribed on the world Heritage List, is part of the "Mountain Railways of India.

THE MATHERAN LIGHT RAILWAY
(Extension to the Mountain Railways of India)

The MLR is a linear Property about 19.97 kilometers long and 0.61 meter wide, which runs from Neral (located at an elevation of 39.31 m) to Matheran (located at an elevation of 803.98 m), in the Sahayadri Range, entirely in the state of Raigad district in Maharashtra, India. Neral is the interchange station, near the city of Mumbai, of the broad-gauge main line in Western India running towards the south and central parts of India across the Western Ghats. Trains run via Neral from Mumbai, and have about 3 pairs of connecting narrow gauge services to Matheran. Matheran means "The Wooded Head" or jungle topped. It is a mountain table top in the Sahayadri Range of about 20 square kilometers with two thickly wooded ridges, rocky promontories jutting into mid air and commanding views of valleys over 2000 feet below. As the morning mist clears, these are revealed gradually. The native inhabitants were wild forest races of non-Aryan origin and predatory habits such as Dhangars, Thakurs & Kathkaris. Matheran was explored as a summer resort at the same time as India's first railway company (the Great Indian Peninsula Railway now the Central Railway) was formed in 1849. After the construction of the MLR, it became a popular resort of the British Raj in India and still remains a well known resort near Mumbai (India's financial capital).

The MLR ascends at an average gradient of 1 in 25 (maximum gradient of 1 in 20 *i.e.* limit of an adhesion railway and any steeper gradient will lead to slipping). The MLR has over 121 bridges (mostly minor), only one tunnel (the one-kiss tunnel), a steep winding gradient and incredibly sharp curves and in the longer trains, the train can be in the form of a semi circle. There is a signage on one of the curves "Ah, what a sharp curve". Over its length of 19.97 kilometers, there are 221 curves, the sharpest being 1270 equal to 18.25 m. This little railway was inaugurated on 22nd March 1907 to enable visitors to avoid the heat of Mumbai area and escape to Matheran (elevation 803.98 m). It is still extensively used for this purpose today.

There is also a heritage steam train service available for chartered train operation. Trains are run at a maximum speed of 20 kmph but on the sharp curves, their speed may be restricted to 8 kmph.

The railway can be divided into three sections as follows :

(*i*) The first section, about 5.57 kilometers long from Neral (elevation 39.31 meters) to Jumapatti (elevation 241.81 meters). Neral was a small village and it gained importance as a railhead only after the MLR was envisaged. Neral has the workshops, locomotive shed, carriage depot and wagon depot of the MLR and all the locomotives, carriages and wagons are maintained there. Starting from Neral, the narrow gauge line runs parallel to the main broad gauge line, leaving the road to the west of a hill, then turning sharply east and the ascent begins. The road and the rail almost meet at Jumapatti station. This station is of heritage significance. The sharpest curve 1270 equal to 18.25 m is located in this section.

(*ii*) The second section is about 11.57 kilometres long from Jumapatti (elevation 241.81 meters) to Aman Lodge (elevation 758.95 meters). Significant locations along this route include inter-alia Bhekra Khud, horseshoe embankment, One-kiss tunnel, Water-Pipe Station (elevation 484.63 m), backward-forward curves under Mount Barry and Panorama Point. The tunnel in this section is located at 10.25 km to 11 km. The stations are all of heritage significance. This is curviest section. There are also four ordinary sidings and four catch sidings as safety precautions against runaway trains. The road to Matheran terminates at Aman Lodge and no motorized road vehicles are permitted entry to Matheran beyond Aman Lodge.

(*iii*) The third section is about 2.83 kilometres long, from Aman Lodge (km. 17.14) to the end of the line *i.e.* Matheran station. Matheran, being the highest point of the line (elevation 803.98 m), is a sought after destination for tourists. There are no intermediate stations along this route. The Matheran rest house, Matheran railway station and turnaround shed at Matheran are structures of special heritage significance.

Trains on this Railway run efficiently for the benefit of the tourists as well as the local communities and offer a rich and scenic expanse of the Mountain area and its associated eco-sensitive zone.

KAZIRANGA NATIONAL PARK (1985)

In the heart of Assam, this park is one of the last areas in eastern India undisturbed by human presence. It is inhabited by the world's largest population of one-horned rhinoceroses, as well as many mammals, including tigers, elephants, panthers and bears, and thousands of birds.

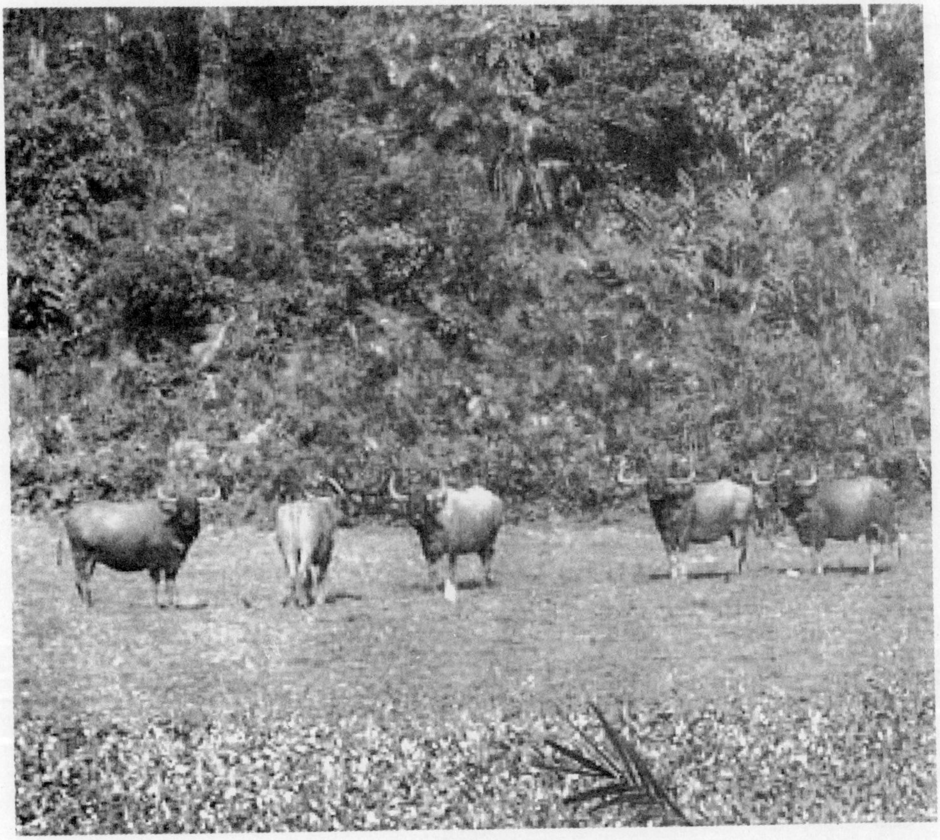

Kaziranga

MANAS WILDLIFE SANCTUARY (1985)

On a gentle slope in the foothills of the Himalayas, where wooded hills give way to alluvial grasslands and tropical forests, the Manas Sanctuary is home to a great variety of wildlife, including many endangered species, such as the tiger, pygmy hog, Indian rhinoceros and Indian elephant.

This sanctuary has been inscribed by the UNESCO in 1992 on the list of World Heritage in Danger.

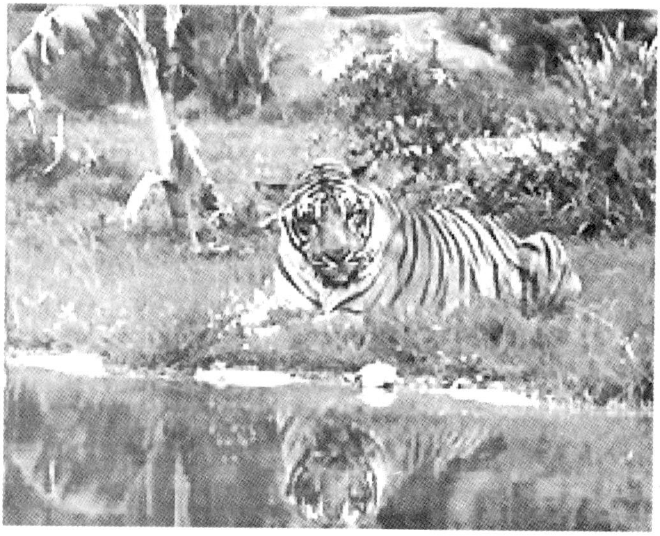

Manas Wildlife

SUNDERBAN NATIONAL PARK (1987)

The Sundarban covers 10,000 sq. km. of land and water (more than half of it in India, the rest in Bangladesh) in the Ganges delta. It contains the world's largest area of mangrove forests. A number of rare or endangered species live in the park, including tigers, aquatic mammals, birds and reptiles.

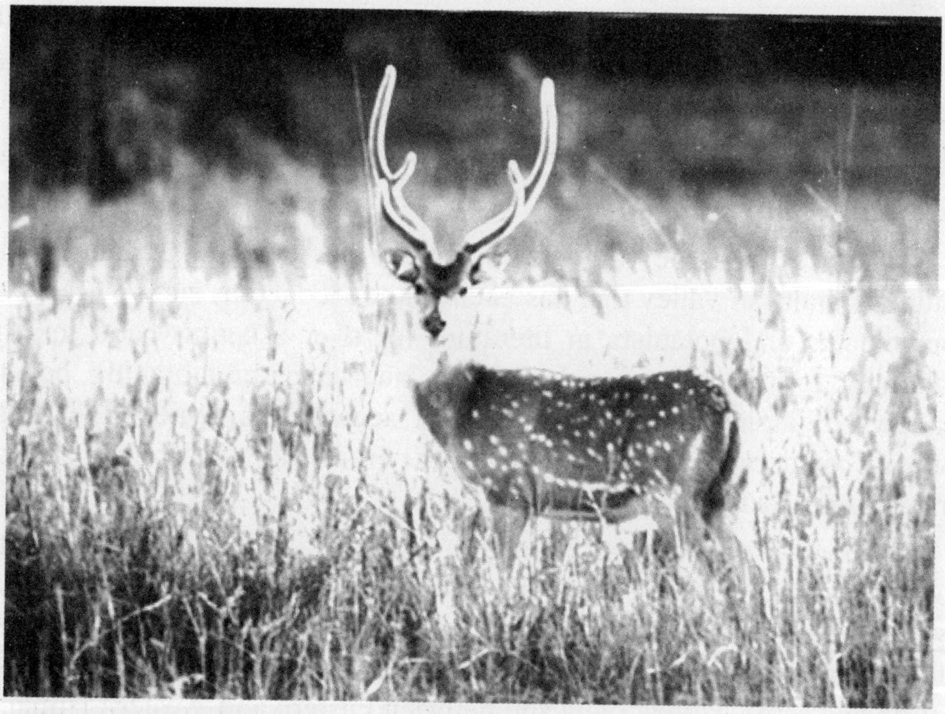

Sunderban

NANDA DEVI AND VALLEY OF FLOWERS NATIONAL PARK (1988)

Nestled high in West Himalayas, India's Valley of Flowers National Park is renowned for its meadows of endemic alpine flowers and outstanding natural beauty. This richly diverse area is also home to rare and endangered animals, including the Asiatic Black Bear, Snow Leopard, Brown Bear and Blue Sheep. The gentle landscape of the Valley of Flowers National Park complements the rugged mountain wilderness of Nanda Devi National Park. Together they encompass a unique transition zone between the mountain ranges of Zanskar and Great Himalayan, praised by mountaineers and botanists for over a century and in Hindu mythology for much longer.

Justification for Inscription

Criterion (vii) : The Valley of Flowers is an outstanding beautiful high-altitude Himalayan valley that has been acknowledged as such by renowned mountaineers and botanists in literature for over a century and in Hindu mythology for much longer. Its gentle landscape, breathtaking beautiful meadows of alpine flowers and ease of access complement the rugged, mountain wilderness for which the inner basin of Nanda Devi National Park is renowned.

Criterion (x) : The Valley of Flowers is internationally important on account of its diverse alpine flora, representative of the West Himalayas bio-geographic zone. The rich diversity of species reflects the valley's location within a transition zone between the Zanskar and Great Himalayan ranges to north and south, respectively and between Eastern and Western Himalayas flora. A number of plant species are internationally threatened, several have not been recorded from elsewhere in Uttarakhand and two have not been recorded in Nanda Devi National Park. The diversity of threatened species of medicinal plants is higher than has been recorded in other Indian Himalayan protected areas. The entire Nanda Devi Biosphere Reserve lies within the Western Himalayas Endemic Bird Area (EBA). Seven restricted-range bird species are endemic to this part of the EBA.

INDEX

W

X

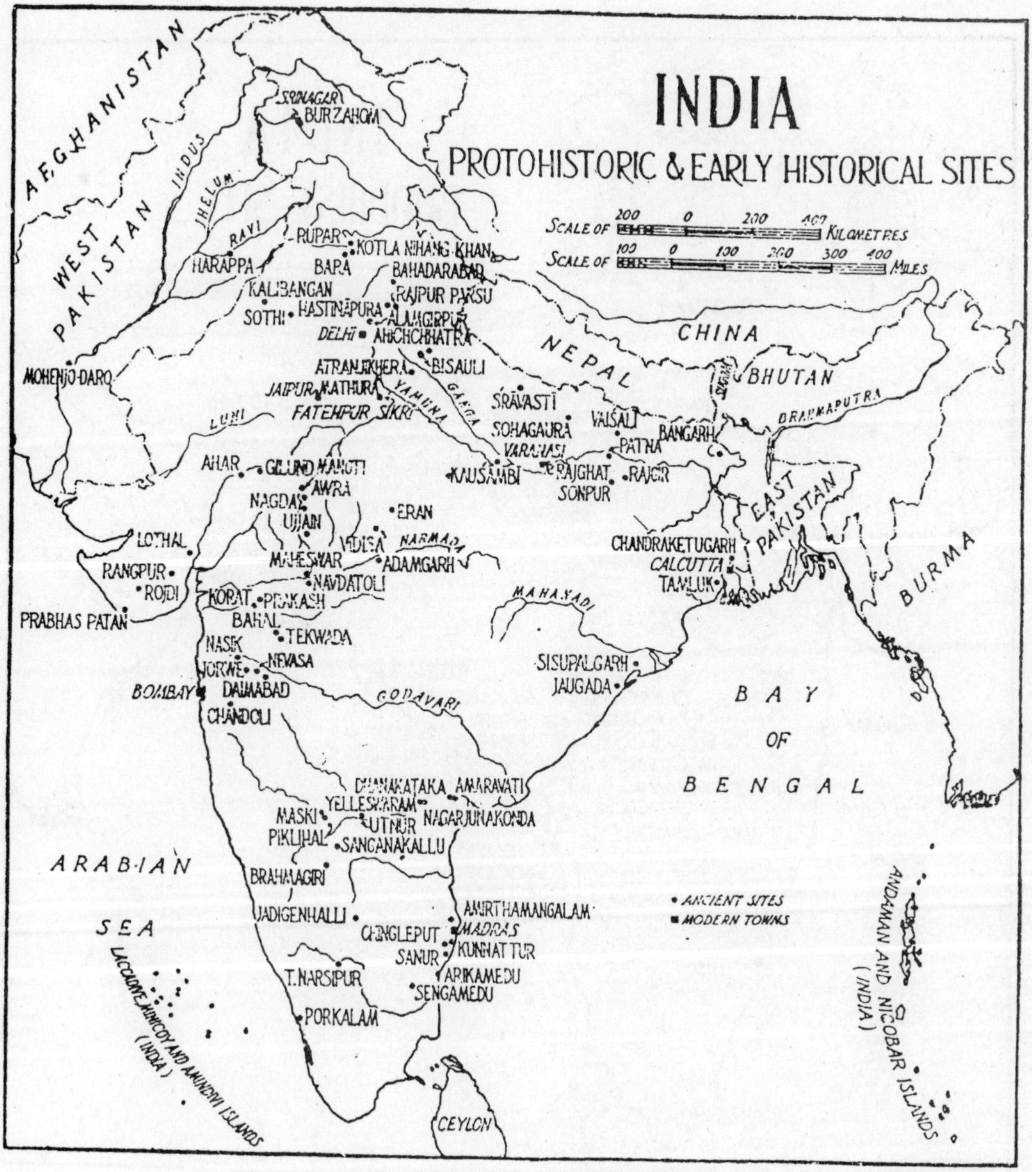

Map 1 : Protohistoric and Early Historical Sites (India)

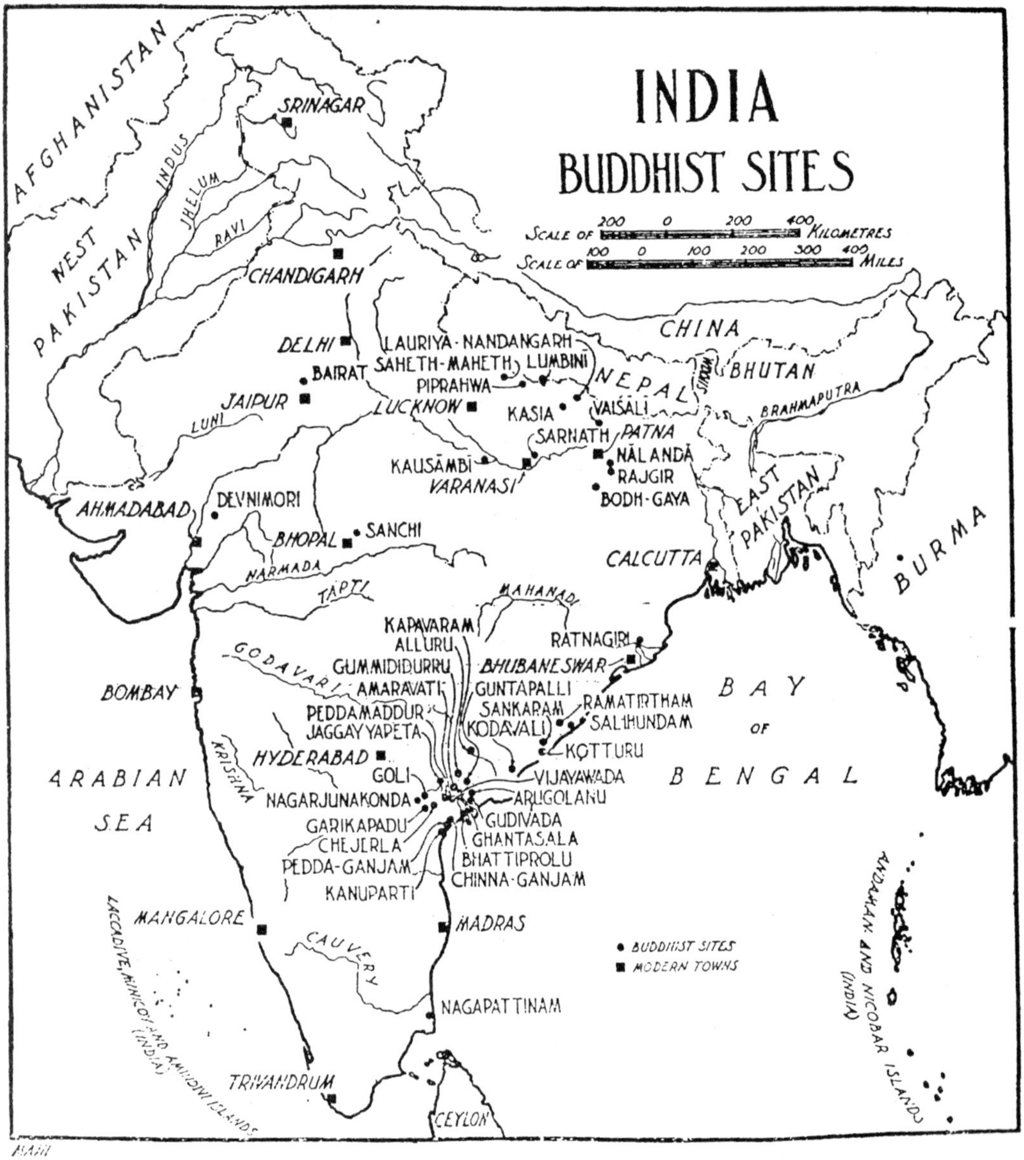

Map 2 : Buddhist Sites (India)

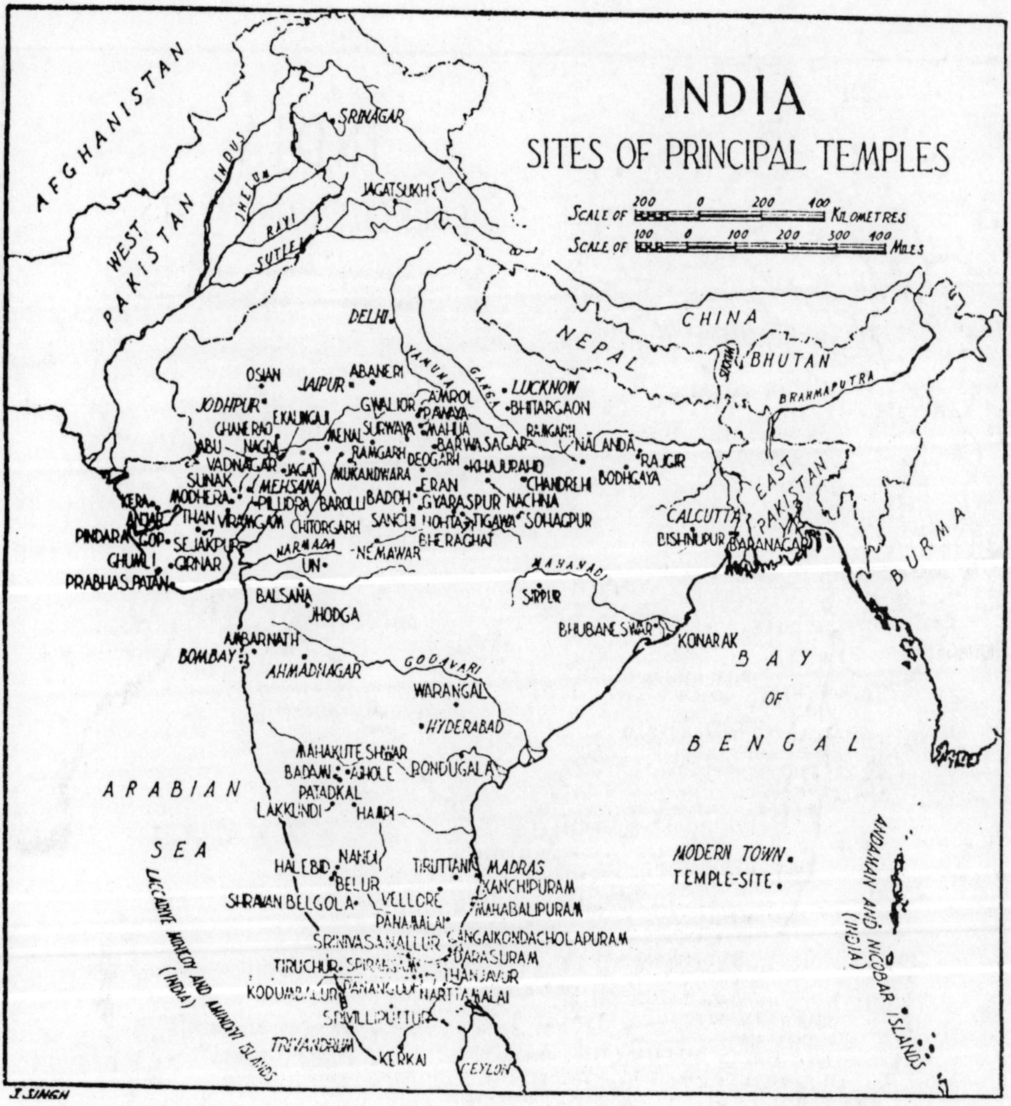

Map 3 : Sites of Principal Temples (India)

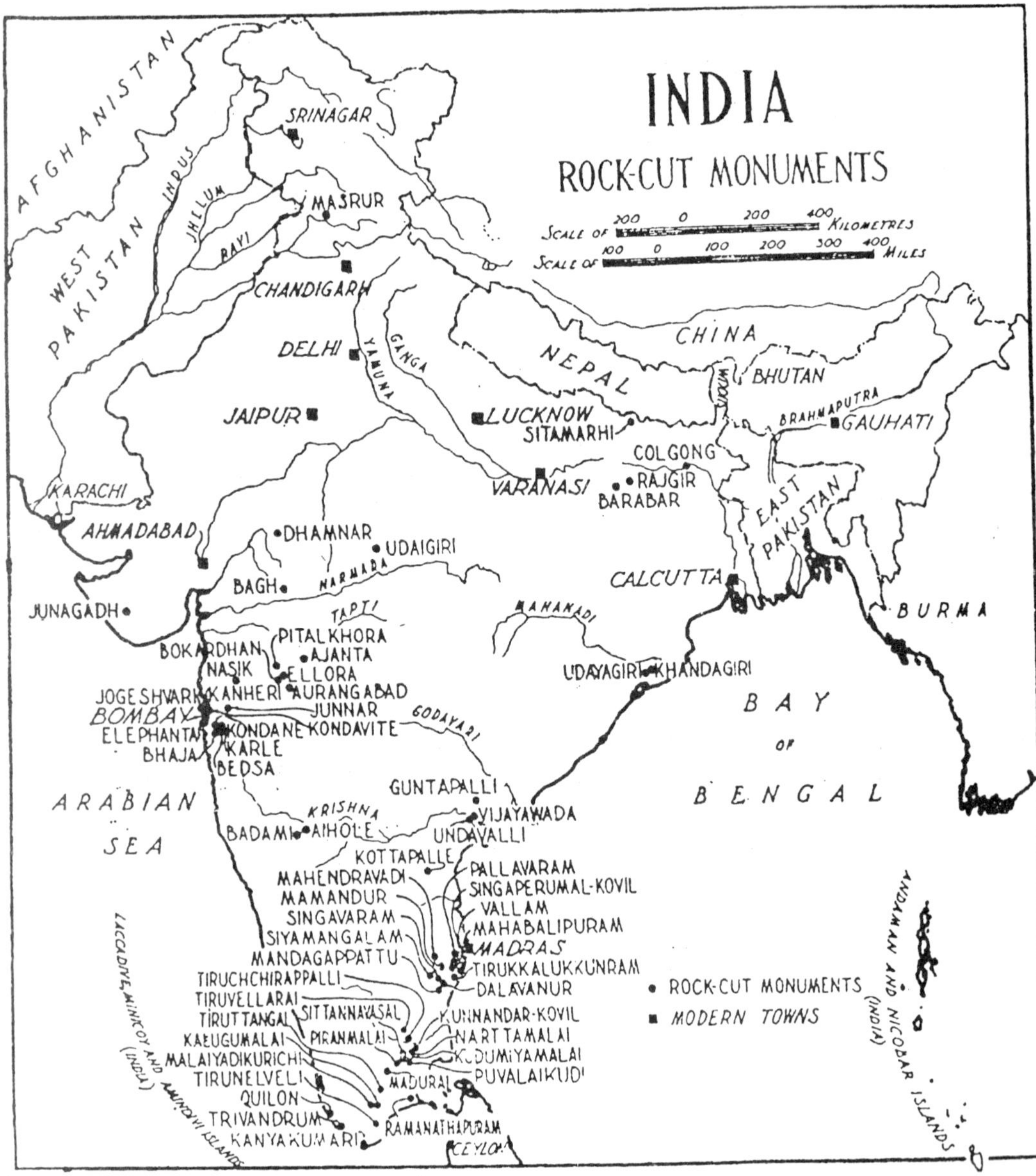

Map 4 : Rock-Cut Monuments (India)

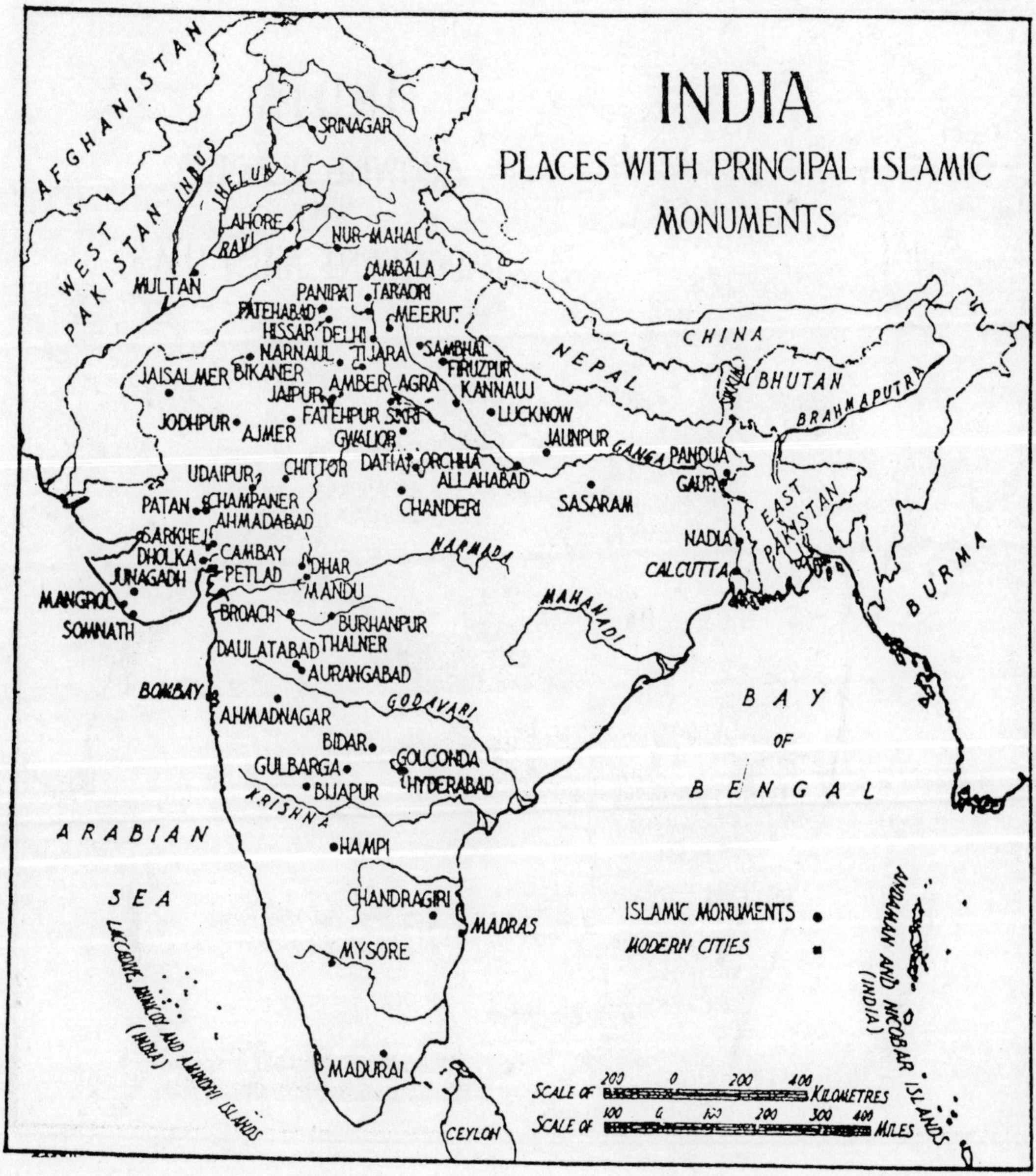

Map 5 : Places with Principal Islamic Monuments (India)

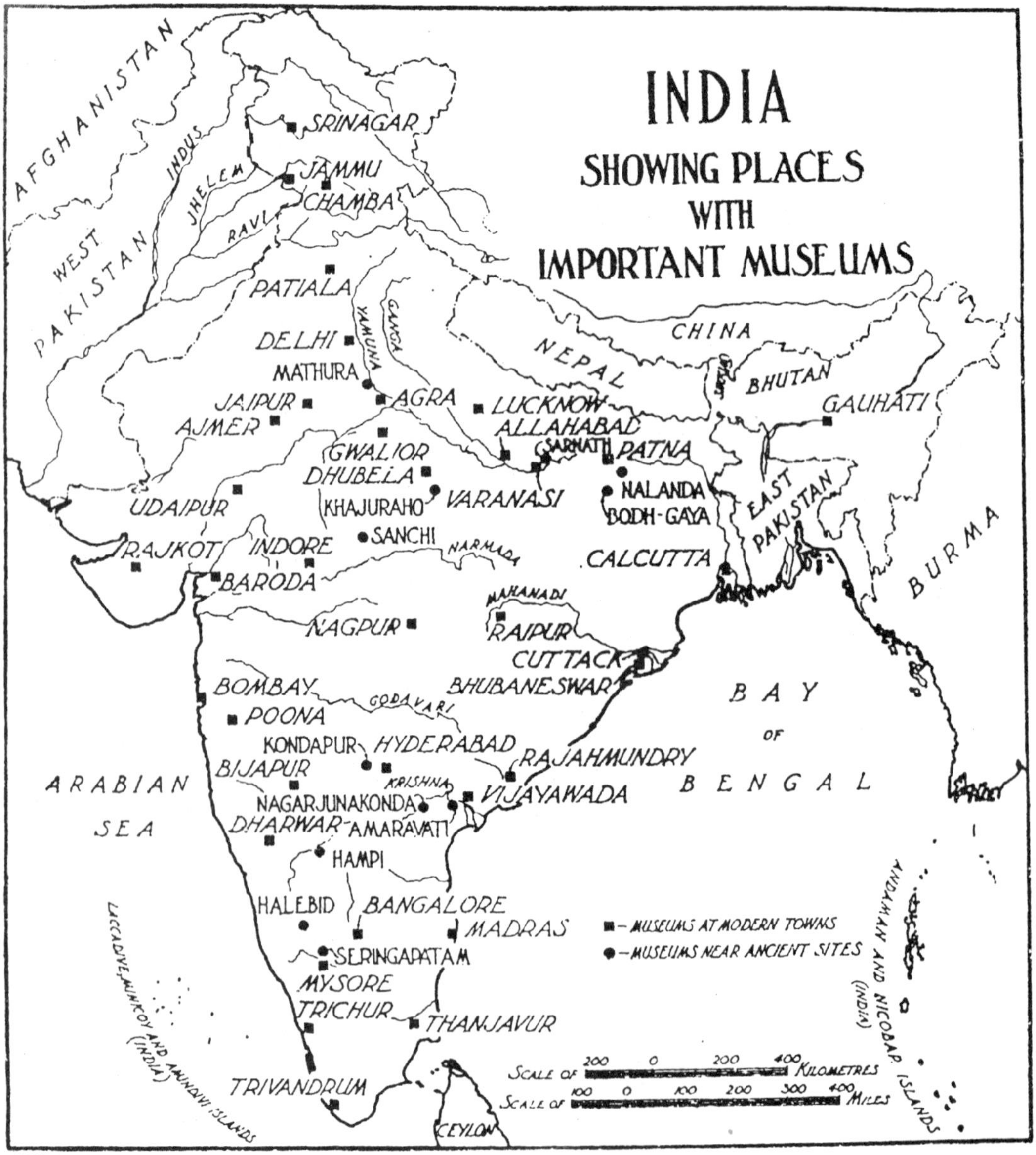

Map 6 : Showing Places with Important Museums (india)

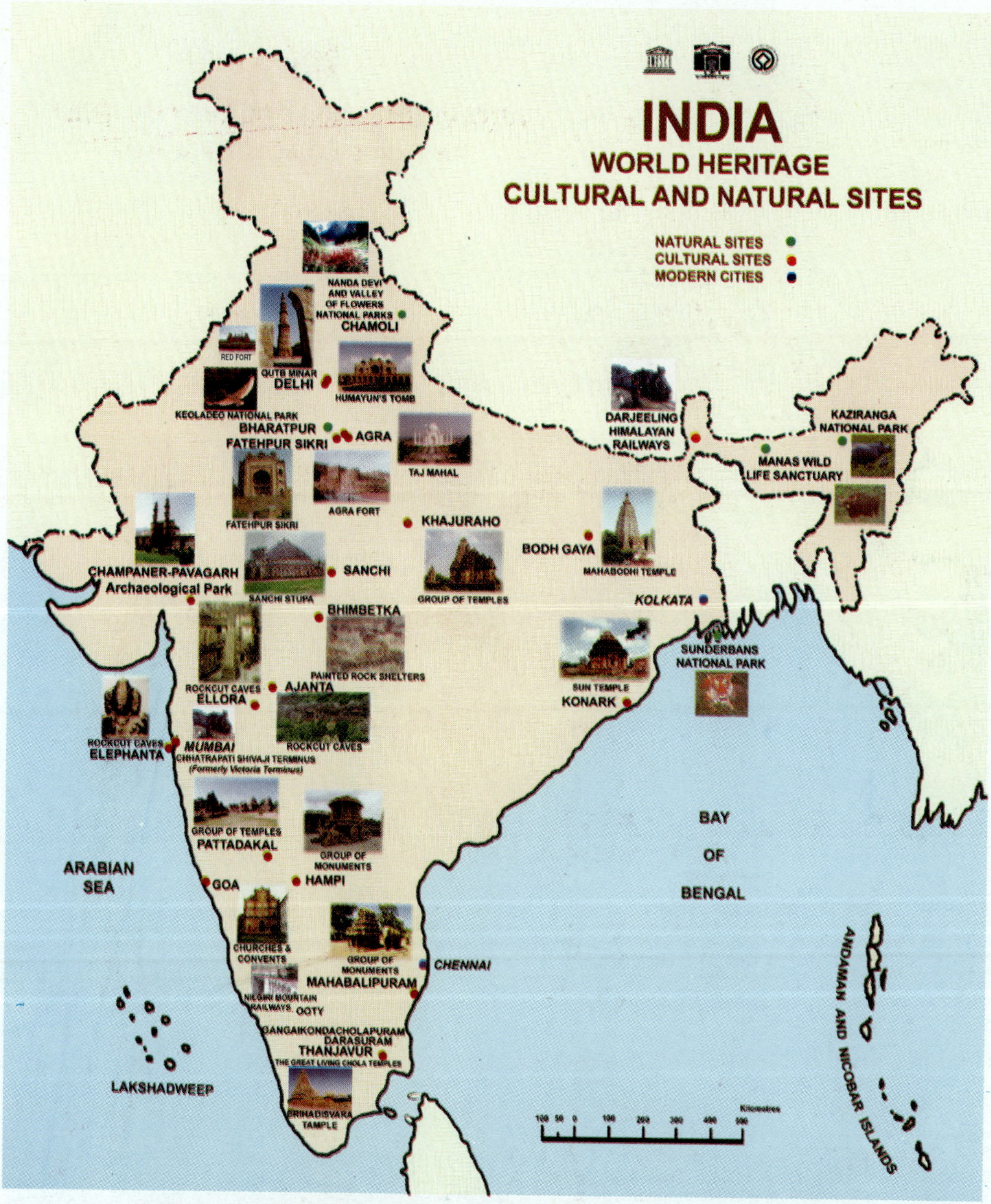

Map 7 : India world Heritage cultural and natural site (ASI).

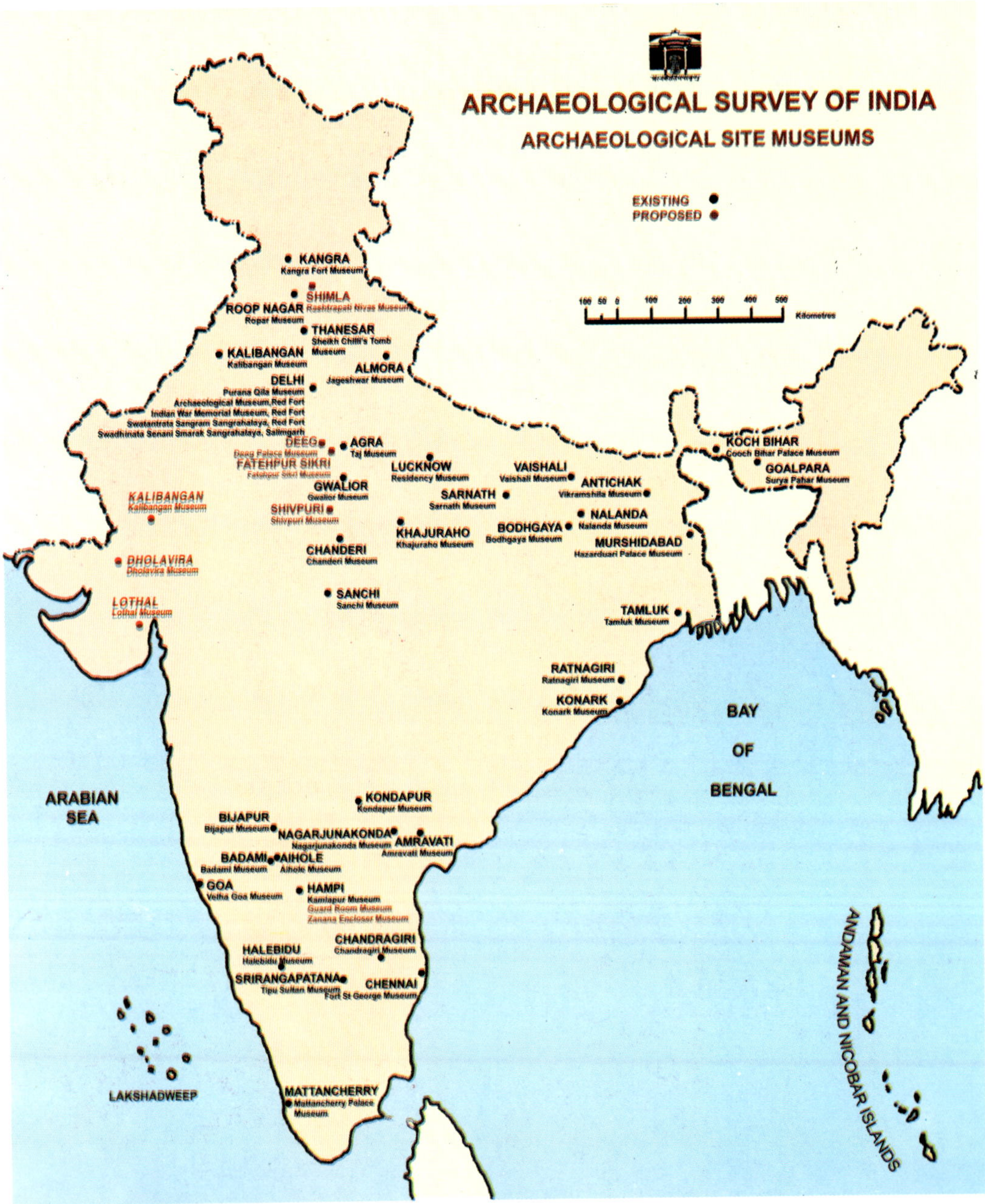

Map 8 : Archaeological Site Museums (ASI).

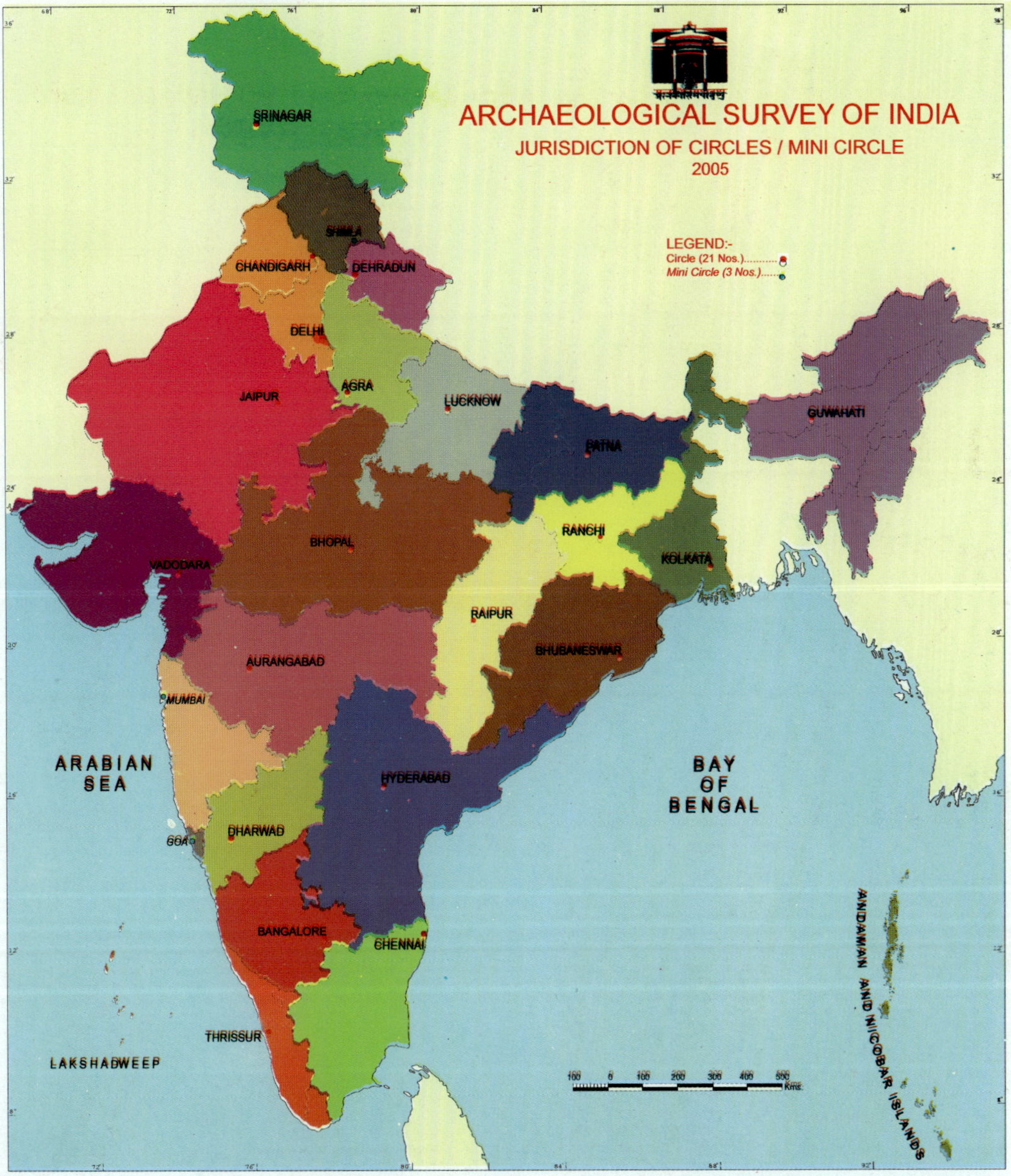

Map 9 : Jurisdiction of Circle and Mini Circle (ASI).

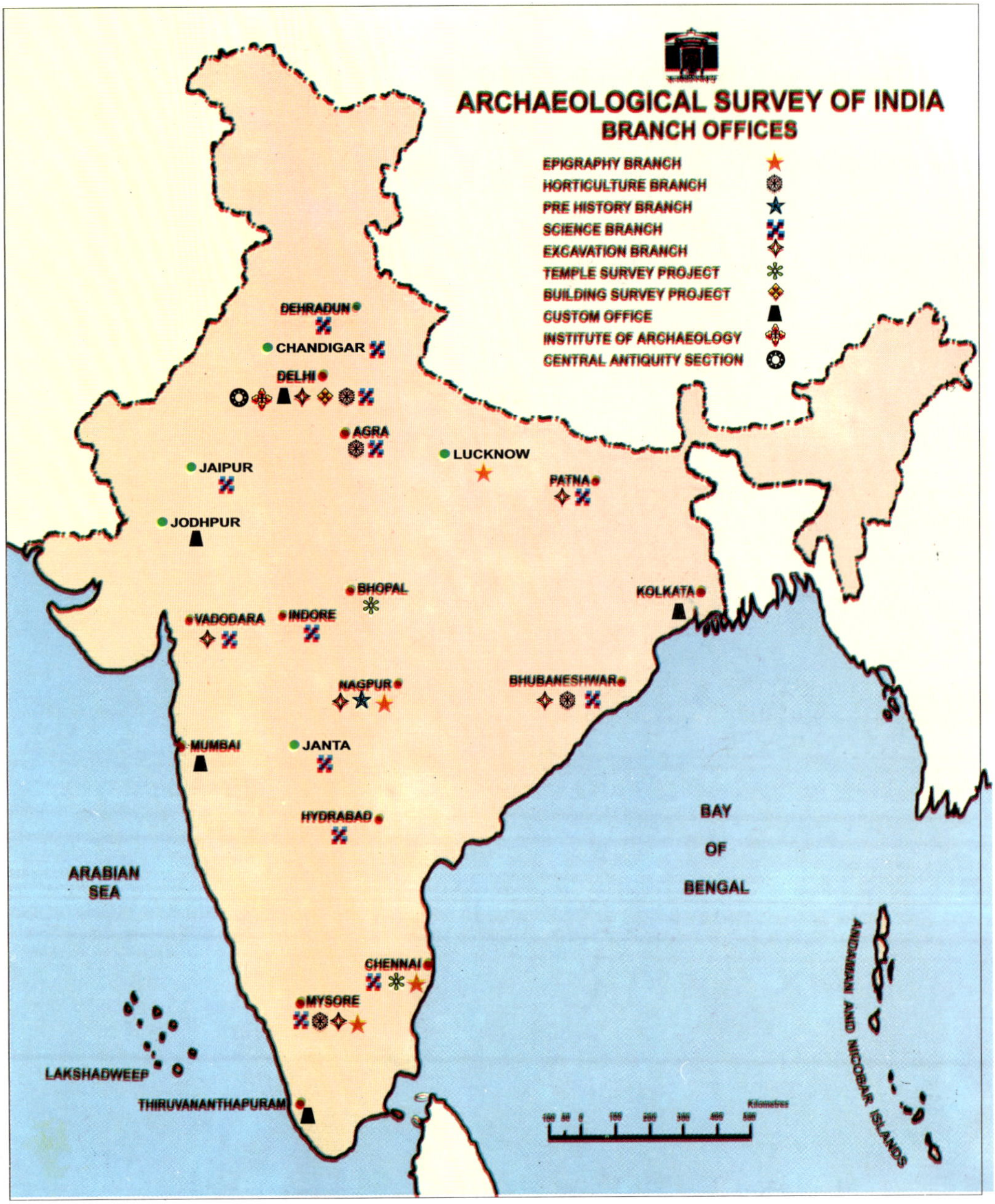

Map 10 : Branch Offices (ASI).

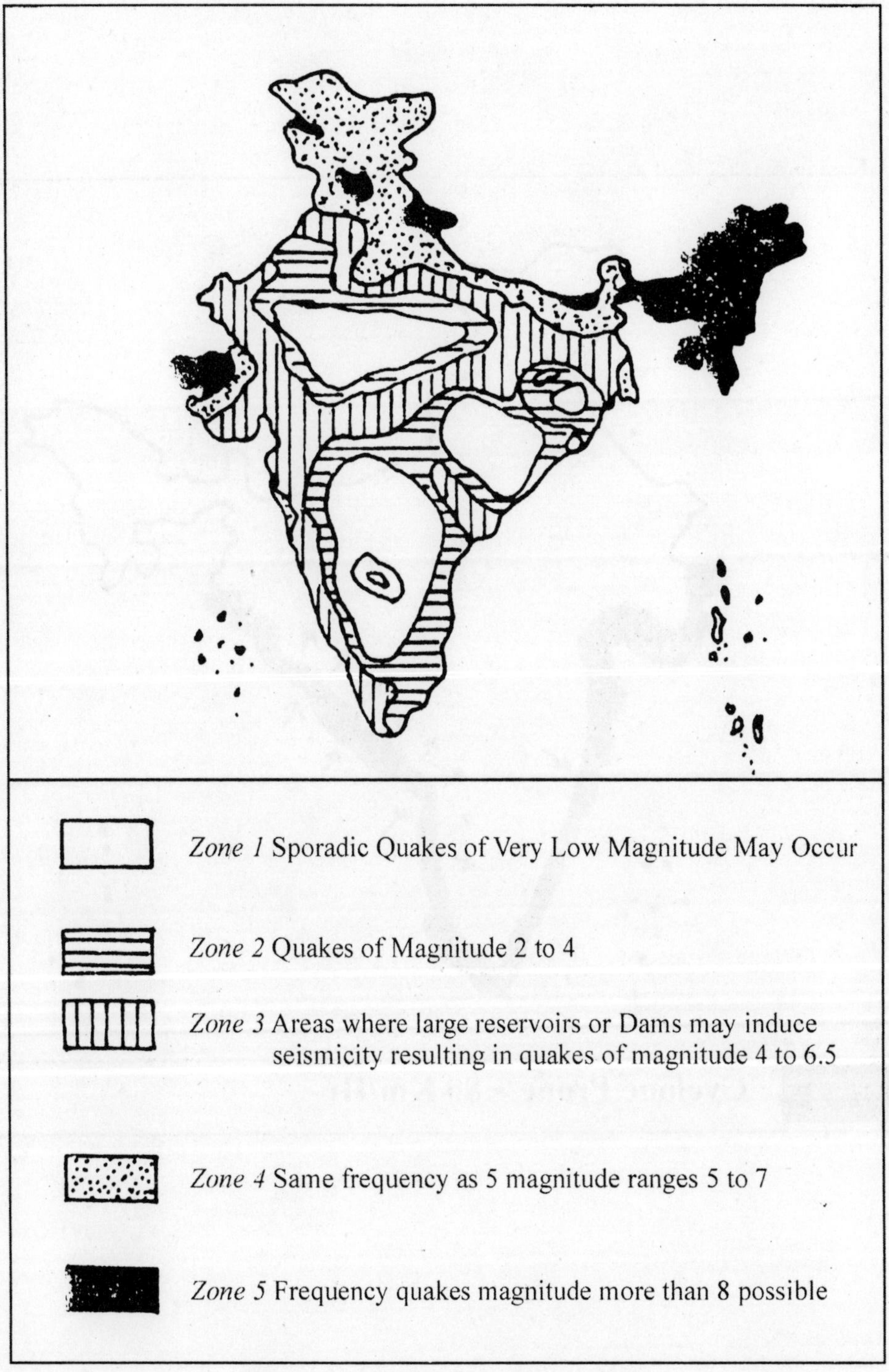

Map 11 : Seismic Zones of India

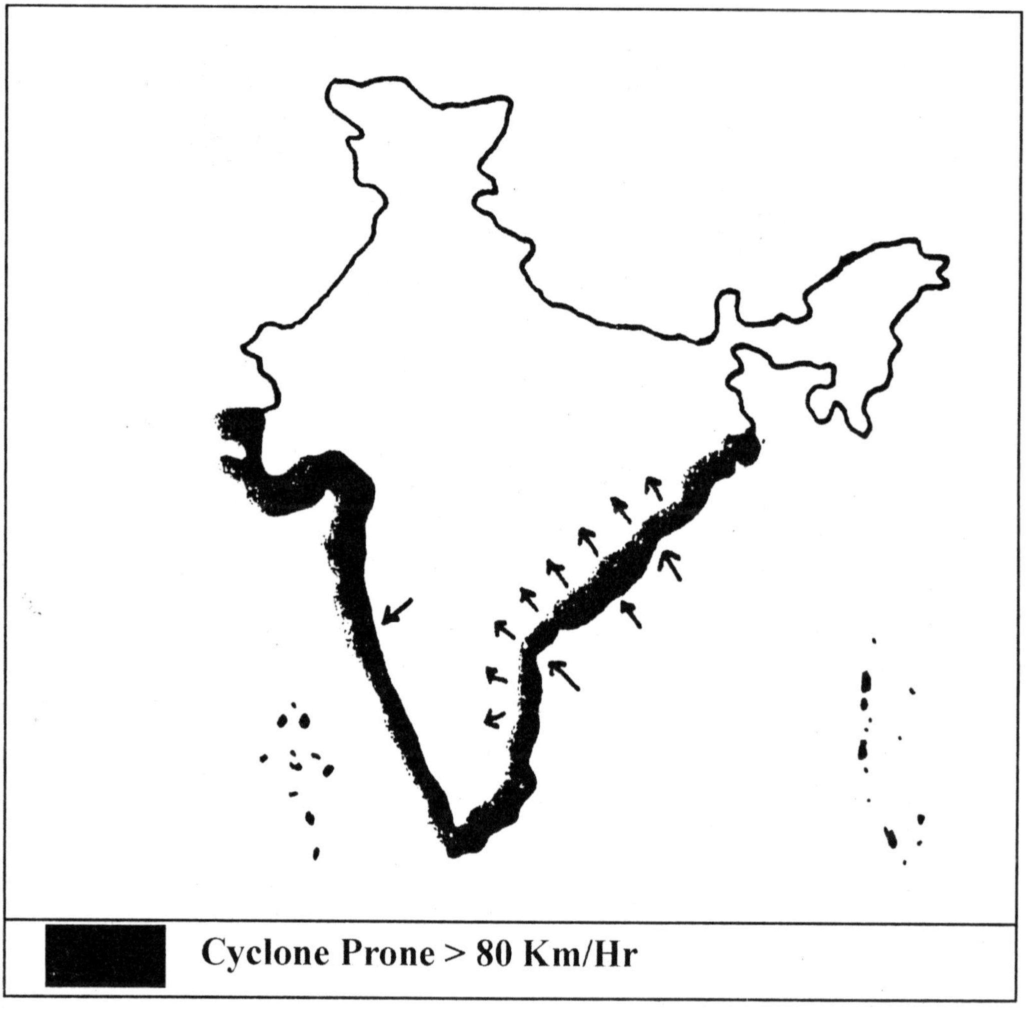

Map 12 : Cyclone Prone Areas in India

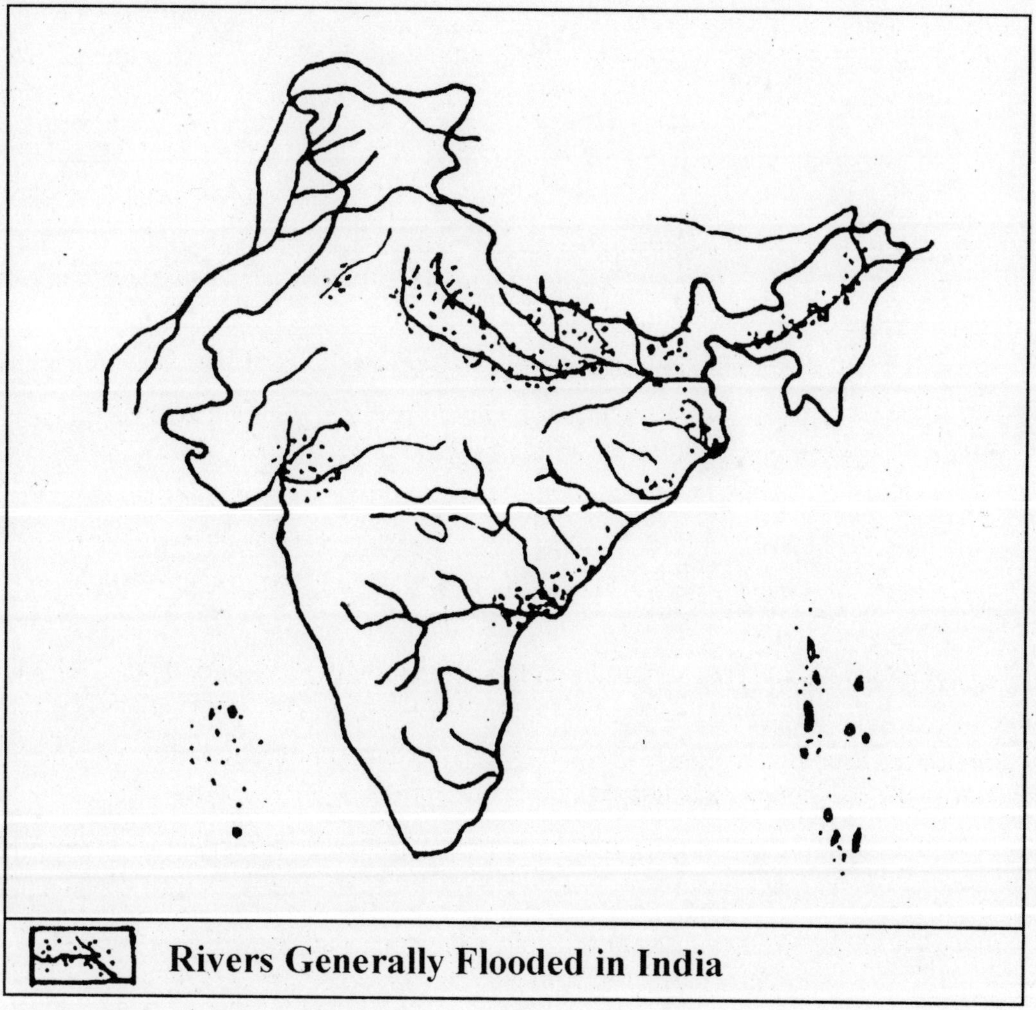

Map 13 : Flood Prone Areas in India

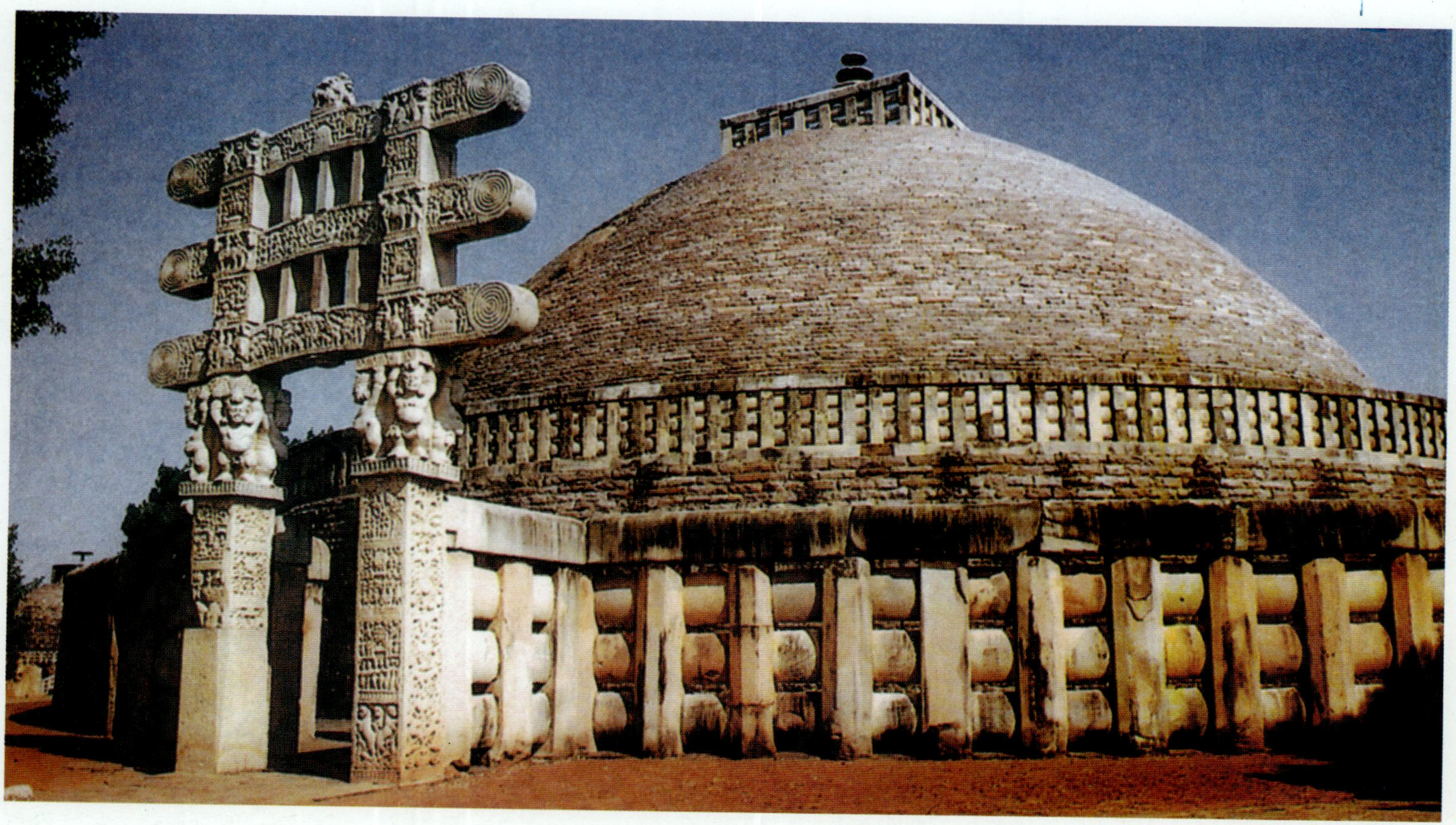

Pl. 1. Buddhist Monuments at Sanchi.

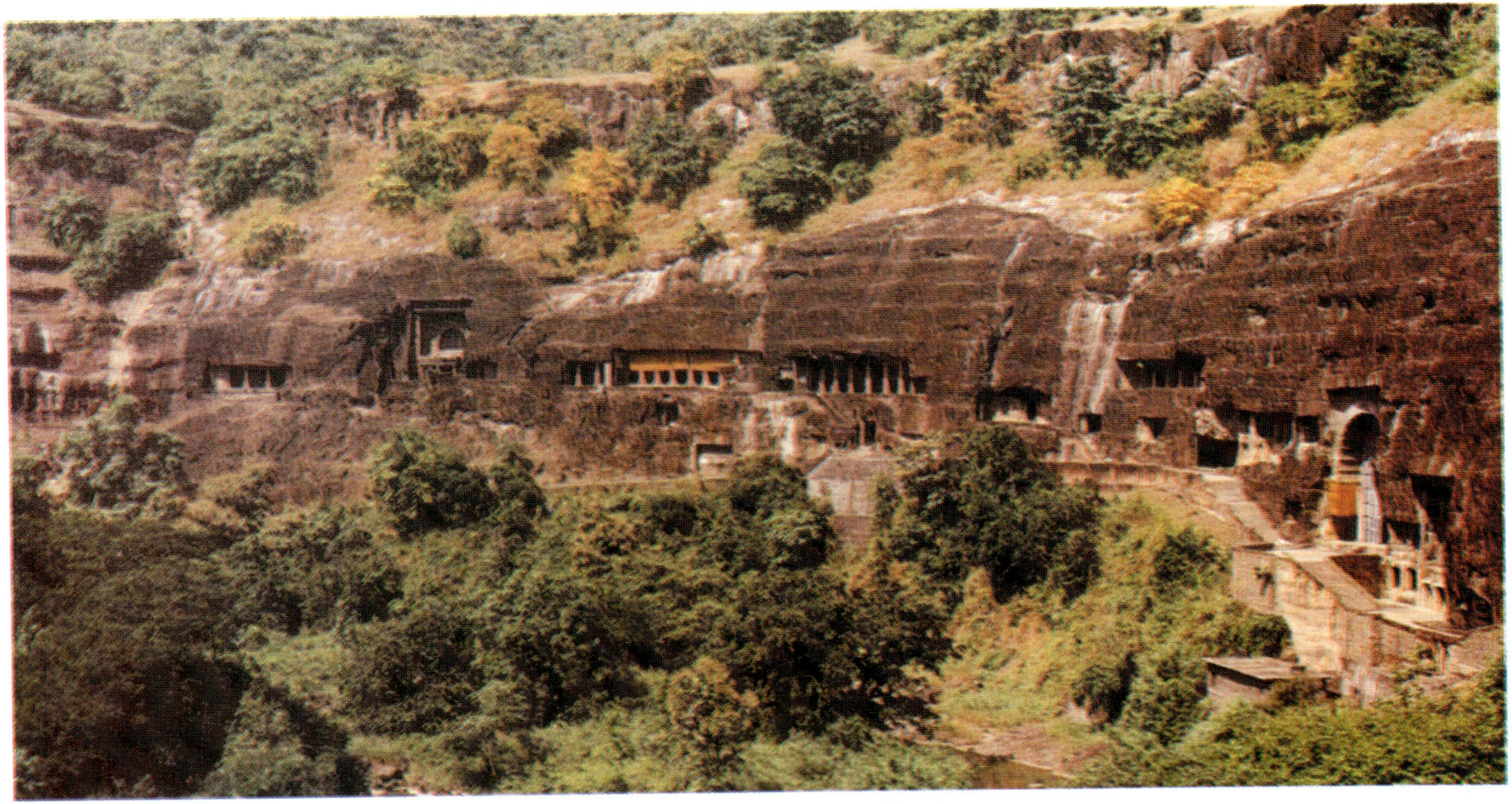

Pl. 2. Group of Caves at Ajanta.

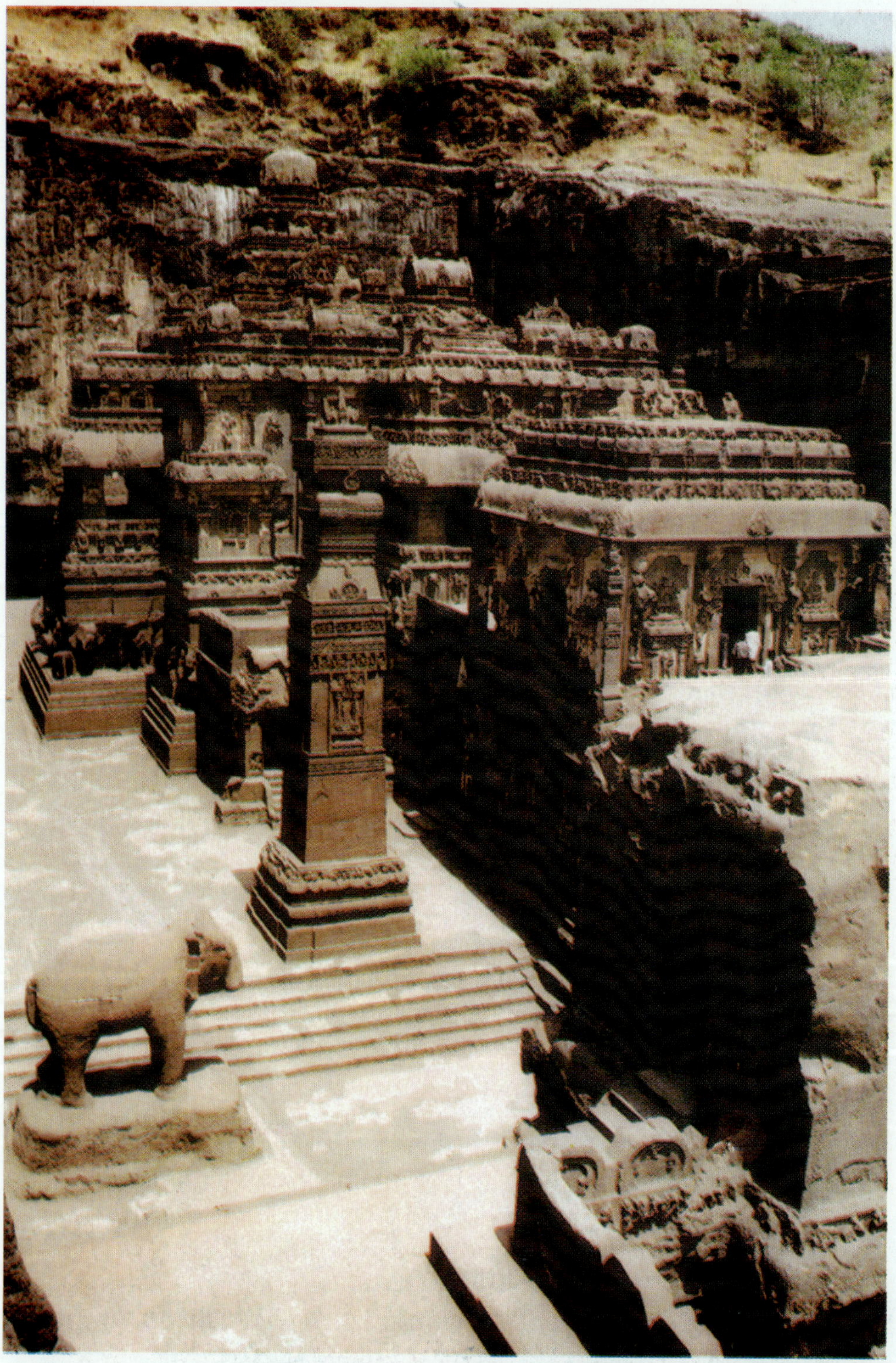

Pl. 3. Group of Caves at Ellora.

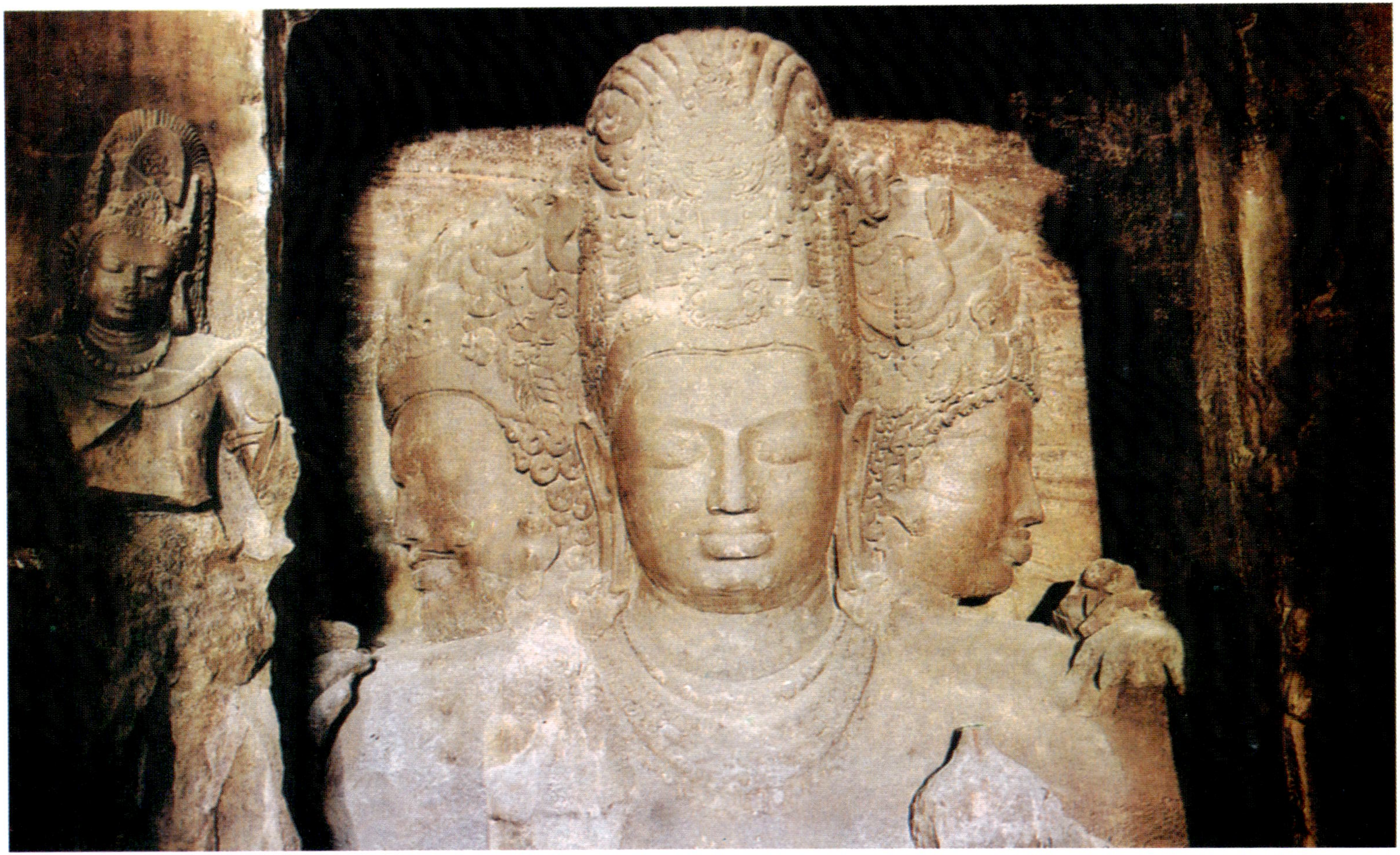

Pl. 4. Group of Caves at Elephanta.

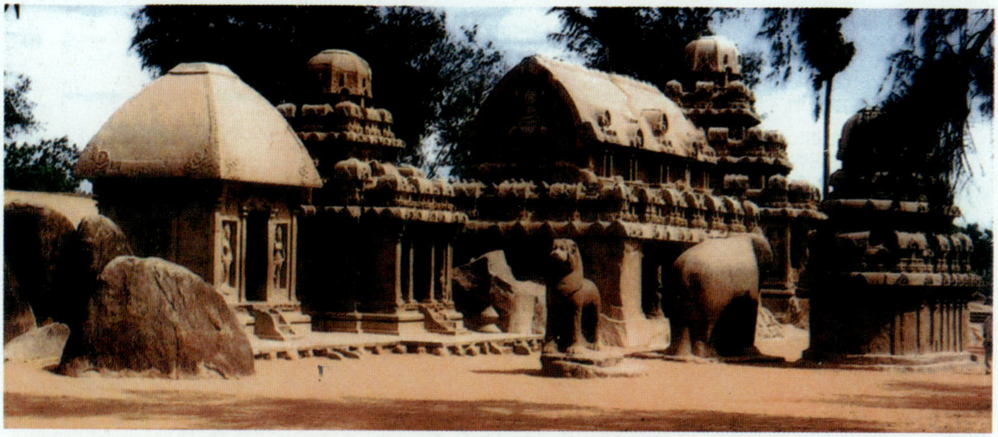

Pl. 5. Group of Monuments at Mahabalipuram.

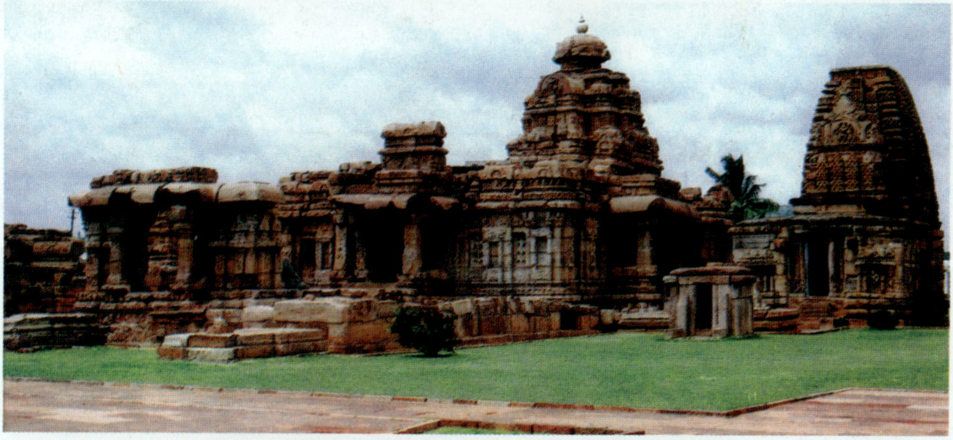

Pl.6. Group of monuments at Pattadakal.

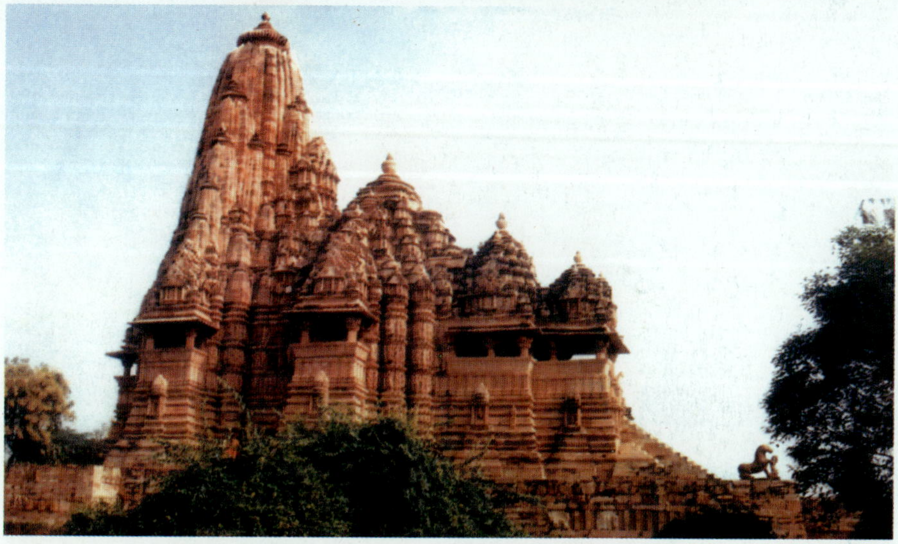

Pl. 7. Group of Monuments at Khajuraho.

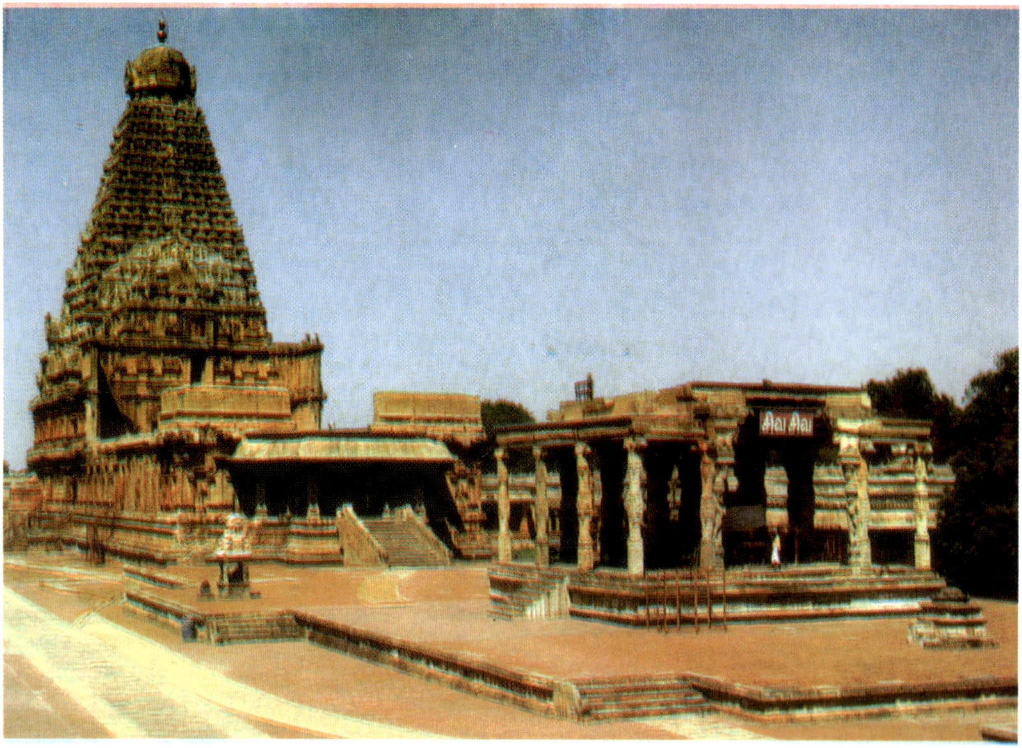

Pl.8a. The great living Chola temples at Thanjavur.

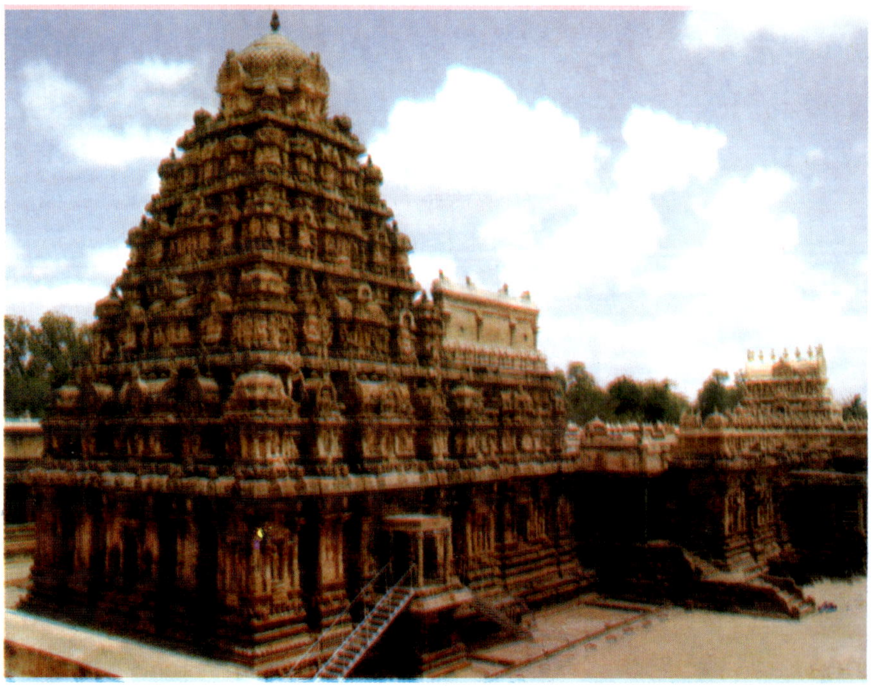

Pl.8b. The great living Chola temples at Thanjavur.

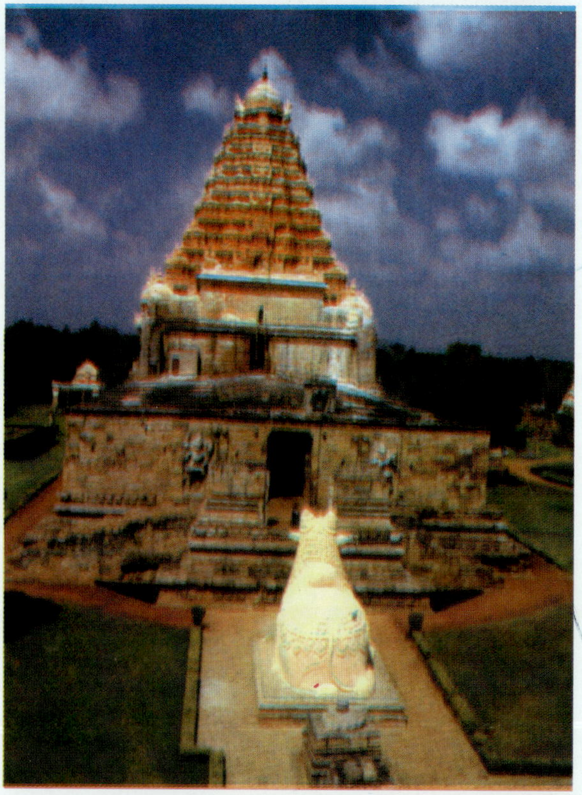

Pl.8c. The great living Chola temples at Thanjavur.

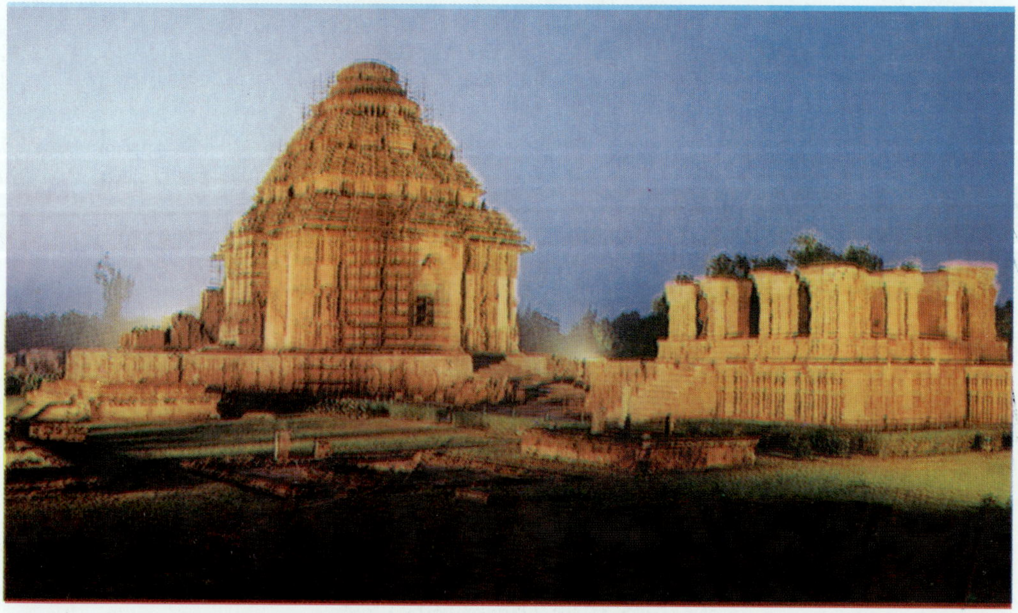

Pl. 9. Sun temple at Konark.

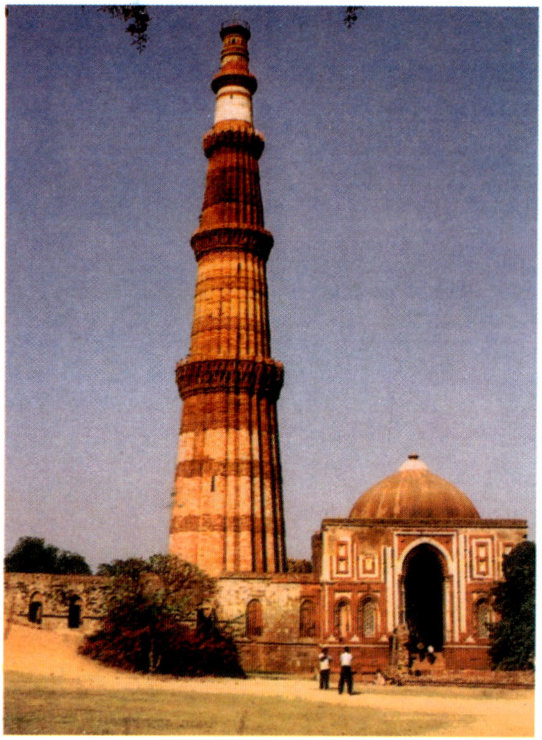

Pl. 10. Qutb -Minar of Delhi.

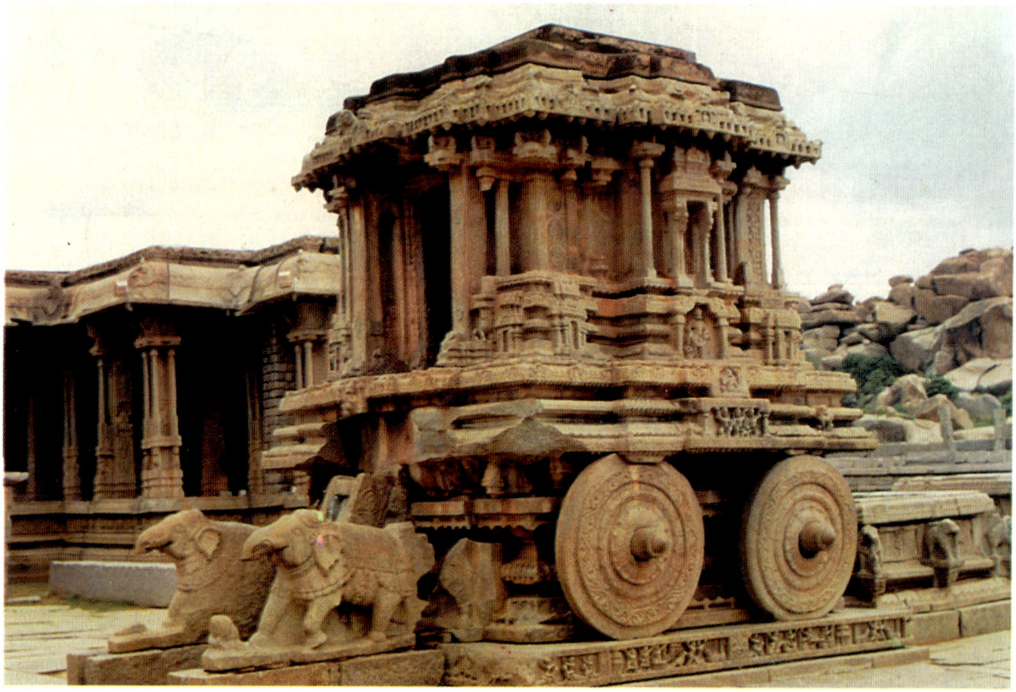

Pl.11. Group of monuments at Hampi.

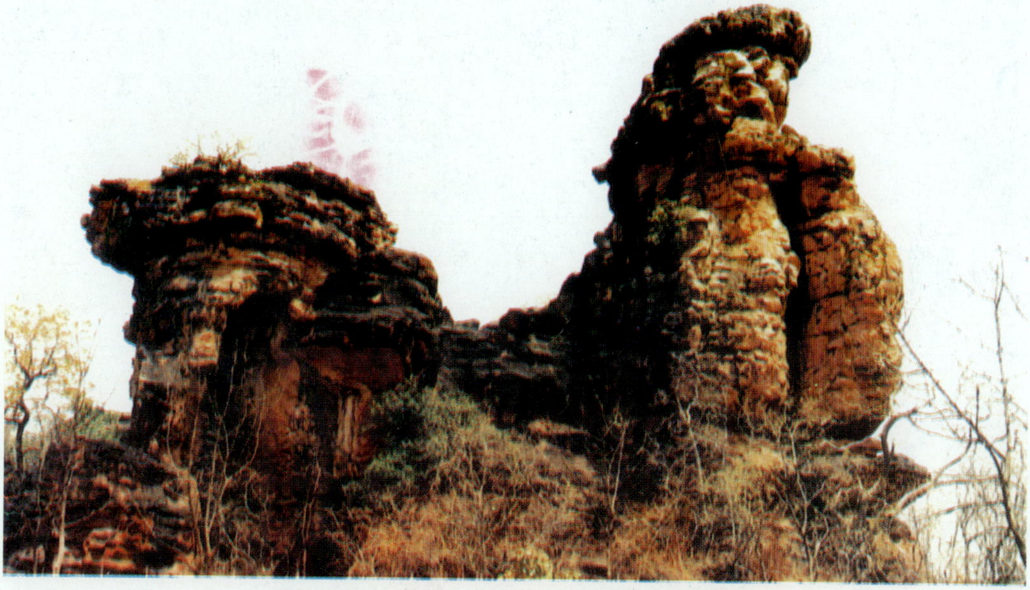

Pl. 12A . Rock shelters of Bhimbetka.

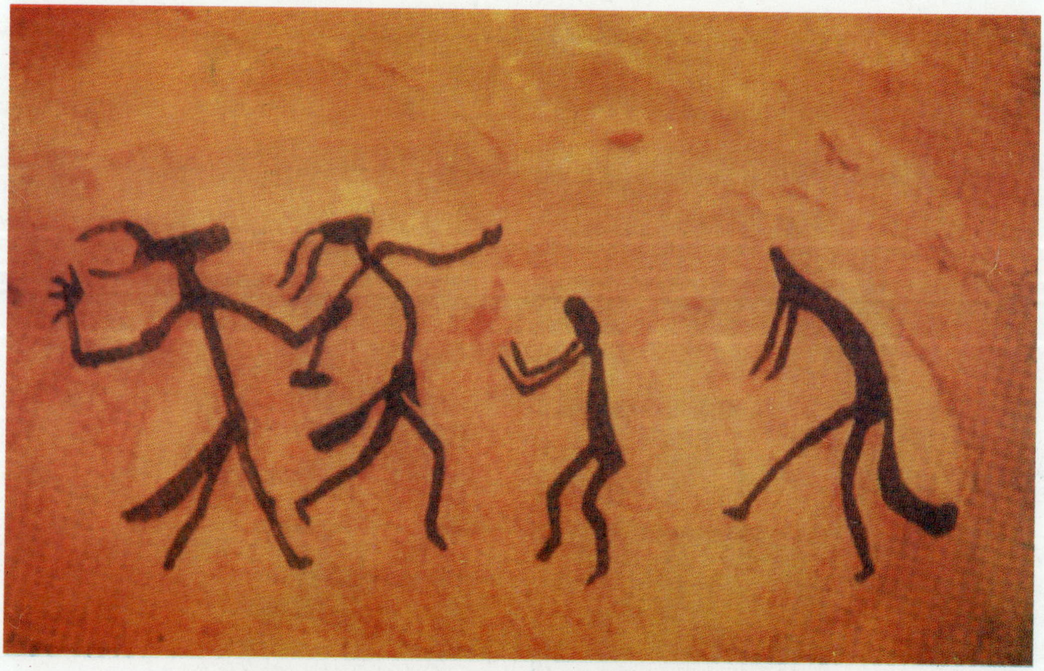

Pl. 12B . Rock painting, Bhimbetka, Mesolithic Age.

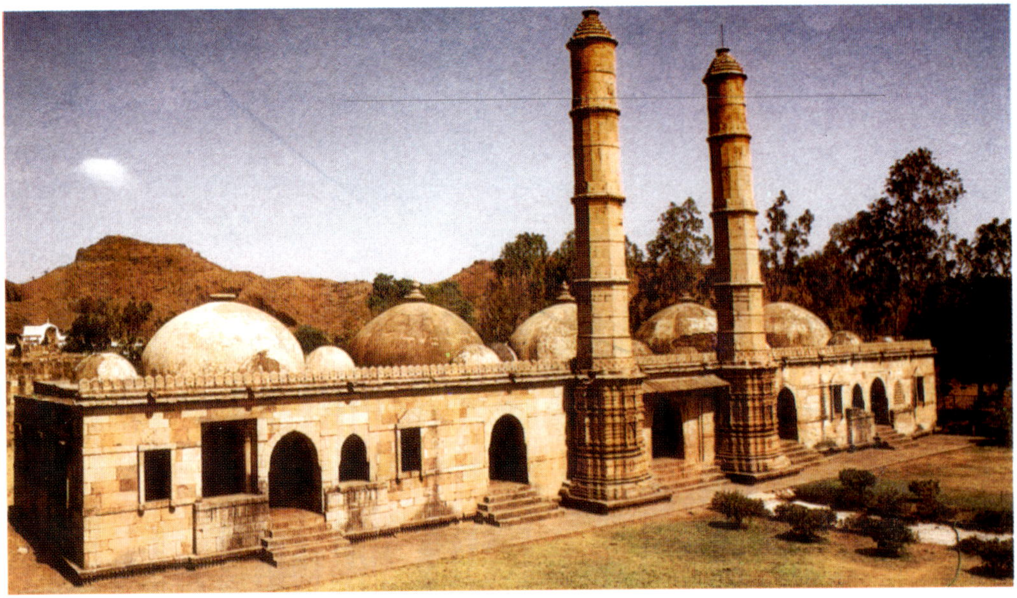

Pl. 13. Champaner of Pavagadh site, Gujarat.

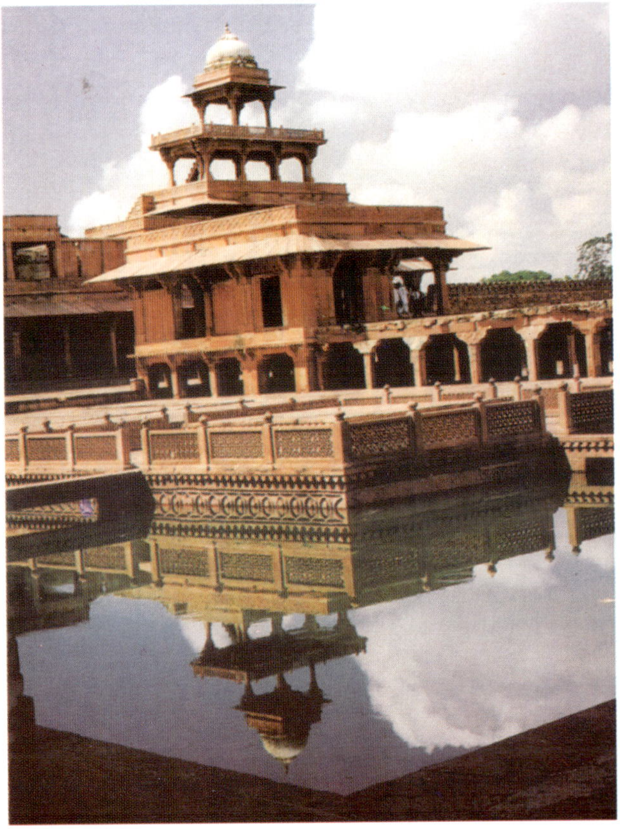

Pl. 14. Mughal city at Fatehpur Sikri.

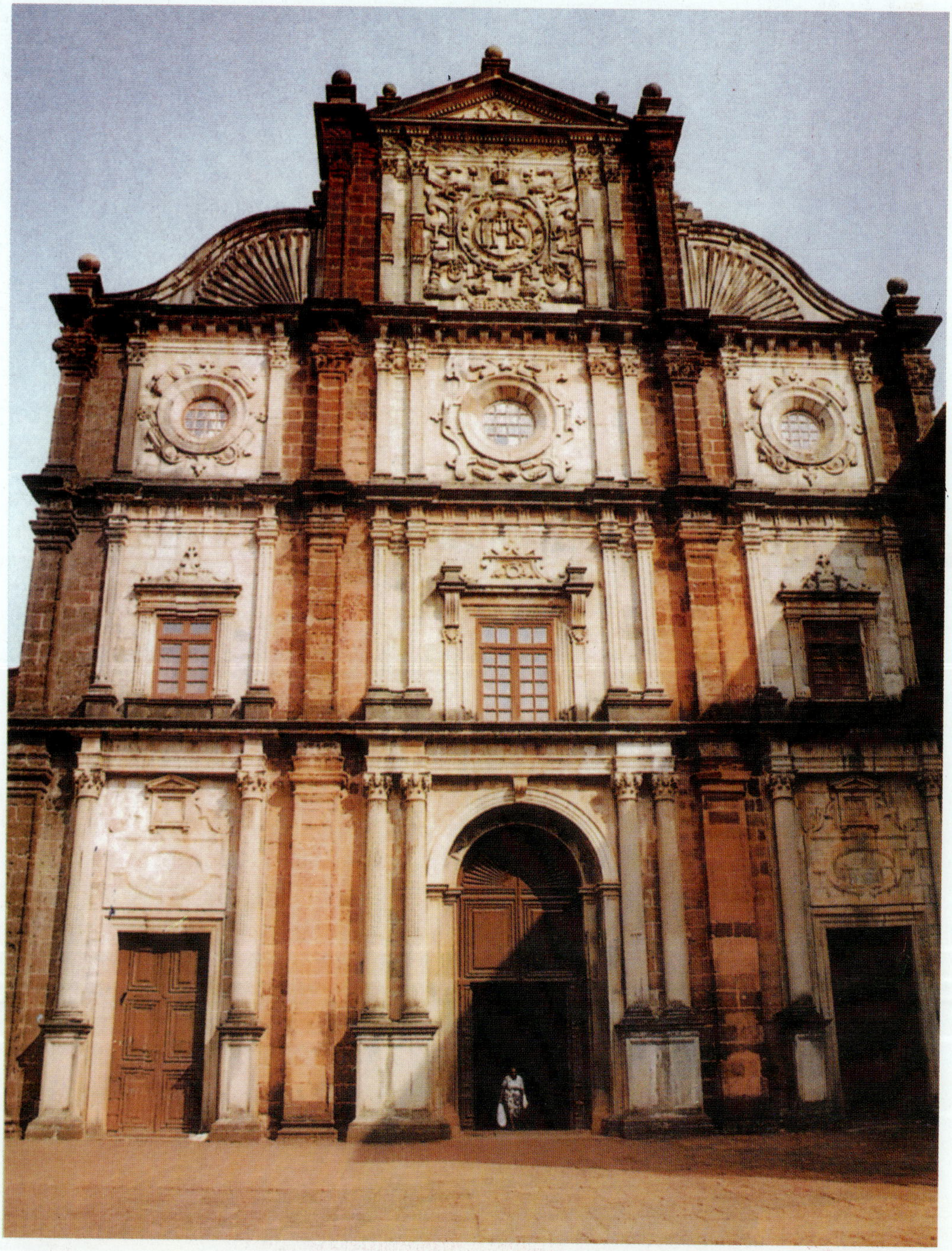

Pl. 15a. Churchs & Convents of Goa.

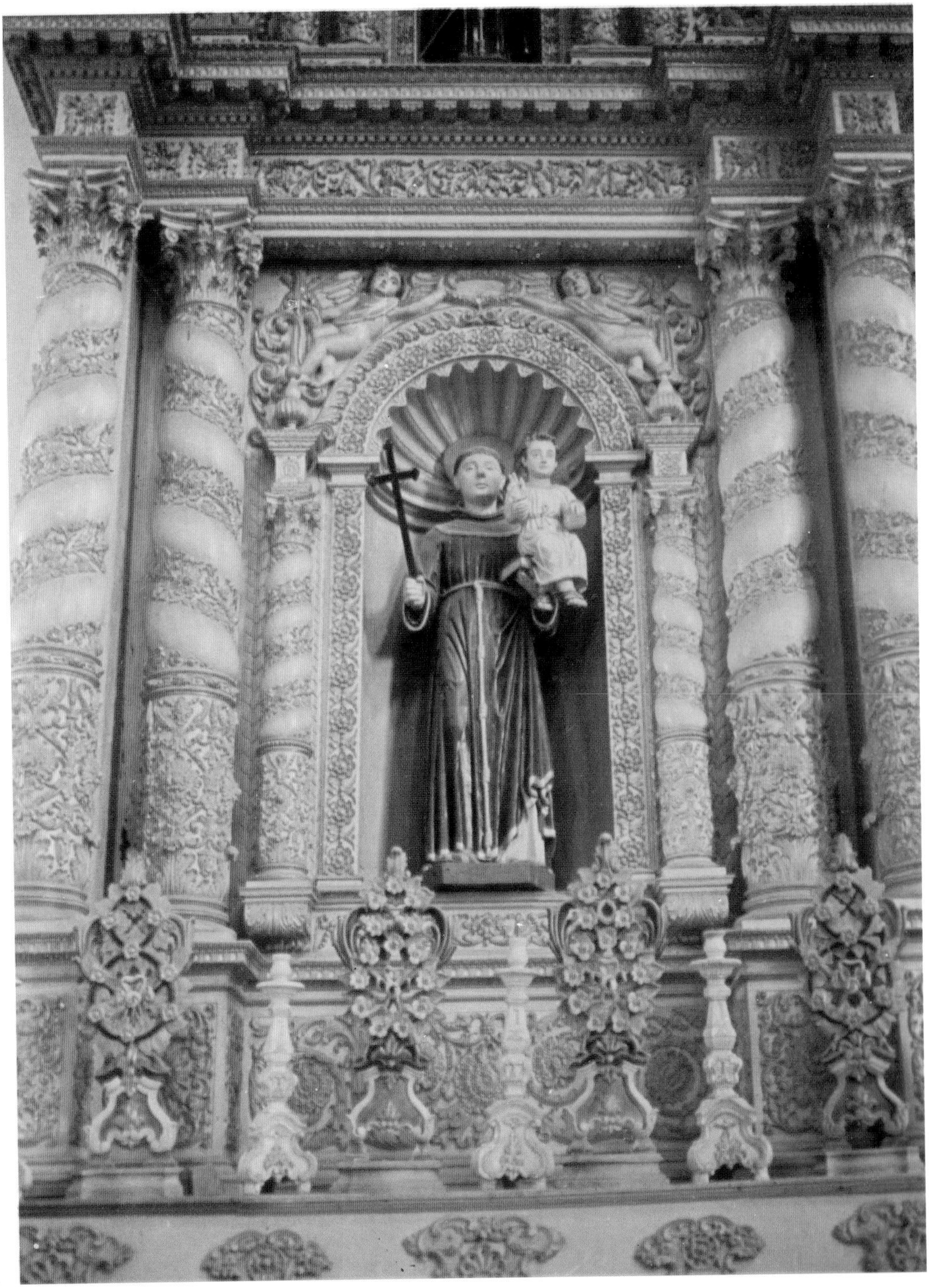

Pl.15b. Churchs & Convents of Goa.

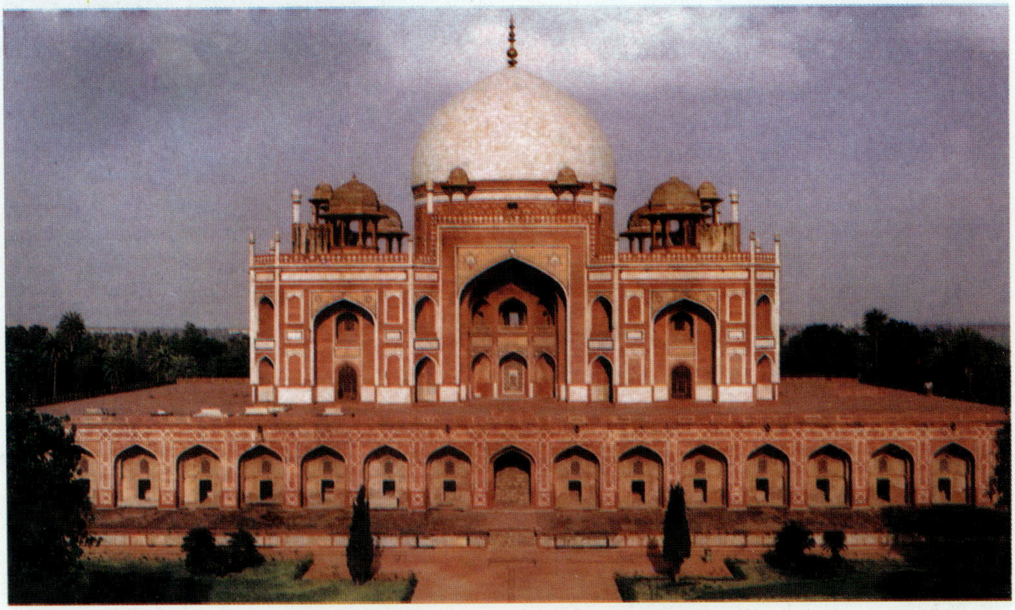

Pl. 16. Humayun's Tomb of Delhi.

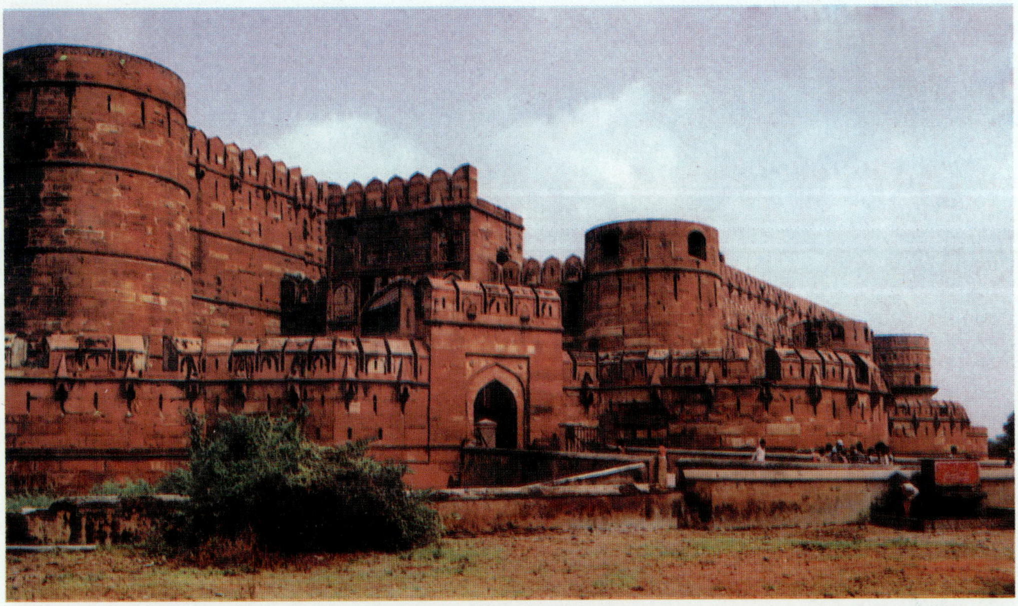

Pl. 17. Agra Fort.

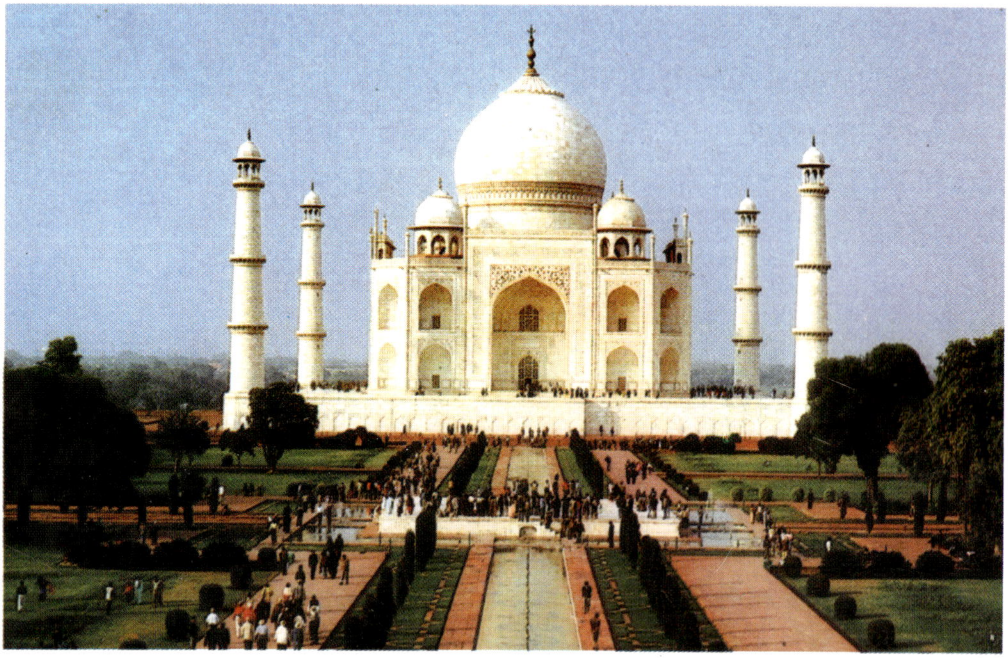

Pl. 18. Taj Mahal at Agra.

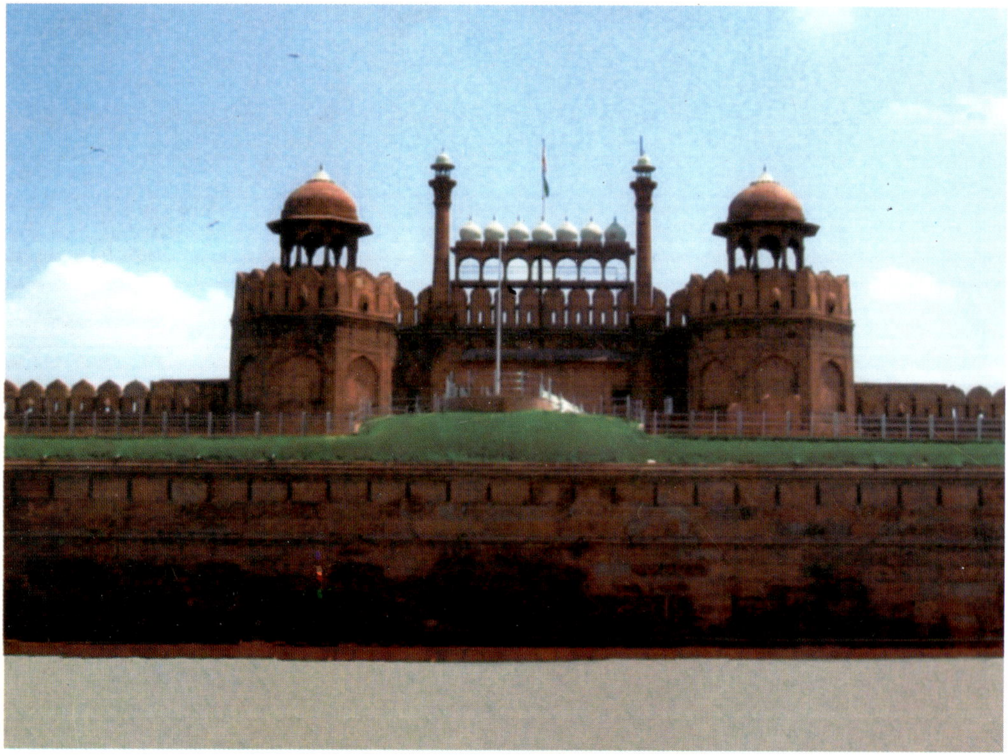

Pl. 19. Red Fort of Delhi.

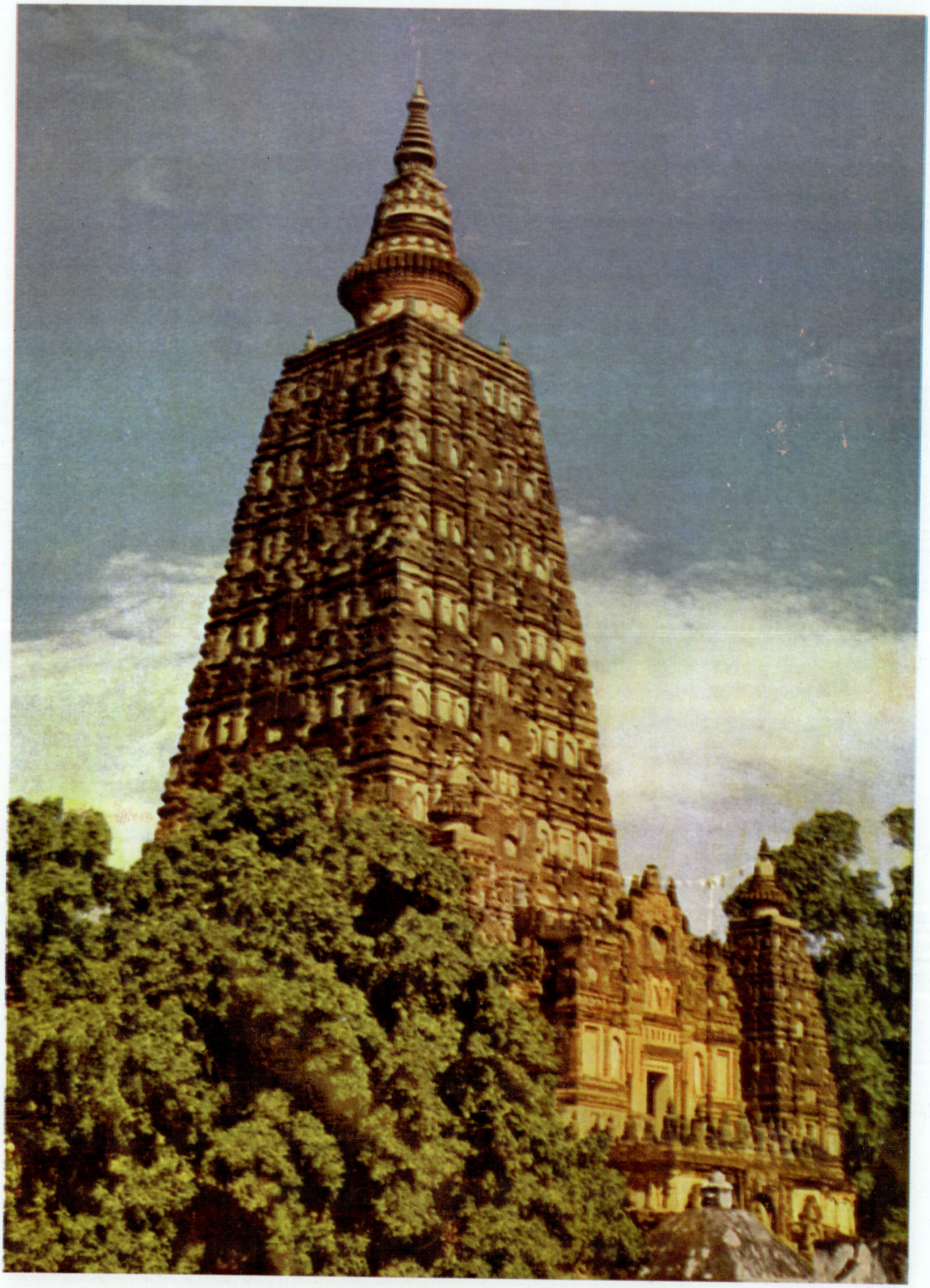

Pl. 20. Mahabodhi temple, Bodh Gaya.

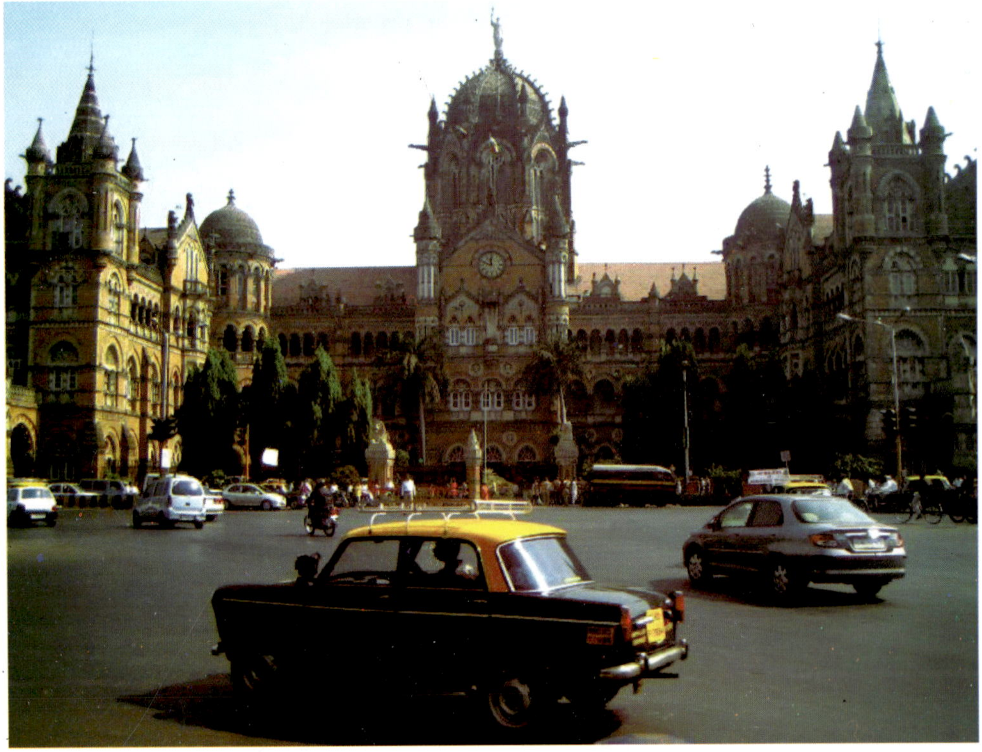

Pl. 21. V.T. Station at Mumbai (Chatrapati Shivaji Terminus).

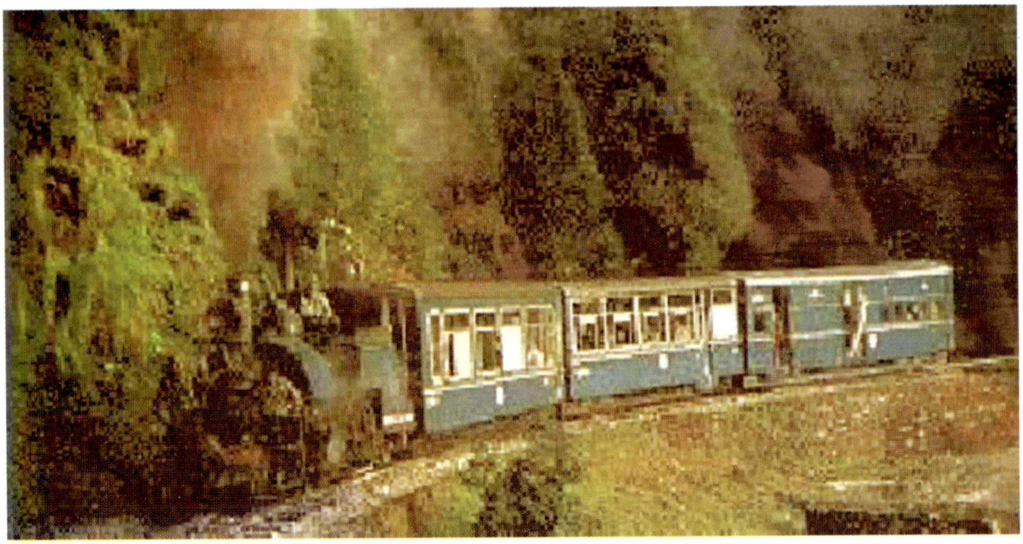

Pl. 22. Railways, Darjeeling.